TRENTINO
&
THE SOUTH TYROL

PAUL BLANCHARD

TRENTINO & THE SOUTH TYROL
Updated chapter from *Blue Guide Northern Italy*

Published by Blue Guides Limited, a Somerset Books Company
Winchester House, Deane Gate Avenue, Taunton, Somerset TA1 2UH
www.blueguides.com
'Blue Guide' is a registered trademark.

ISBN 978-1905131-65-5

The first ever Blue Guide, *London and its Environs,* was published in 1918 by two
Scottish brothers, James and Findlay Muirhead. The first edition of Blue Guide
Northern Italy was compiled by them and L.V. Bertarelli in 1924. Subsequent
editions were revised, compiled or written by the Muirhead brothers (1927, 1937);
Stuart Rossiter (1971); Alta Macadam (1978, 1984, 1991, 1998) and Paul Blanchard
(2001, 2005). This chapter was updated by Paul Blanchard.

The author and publisher have made reasonable efforts to ensure the accuracy of
all the information in this book; however, they can accept no responsibility for any
loss, injury or inconvenience sustained by any traveller as a result of information
or advice contained in the guide.

Every effort has been made to trace the copyright owners of material reproduced
in this guide. We would be pleased to hear from any copyright owners we have been
unable to reach.

Statement of editorial independence: Blue Guides, their authors and editors, are
prohibited from accepting payment from any restaurant, hotel, gallery or other
establishment for its inclusion in this guide or on www.blueguides.com, or for a
more favourable mention than would otherwise have been made.

Town plans © Blue Guides
Maps: Dimap Bt. © Blue Guides
Prepared for press by Anikó Kuzmich.
Cover image: Peaks of the Dolomites © Paul Blanchard

www.blueguides.com
'Blue Guide' is a registered trademark.
We welcome reader comments, questions and feedback:
editorial@blueguides.com.

About the author:
Paul Blanchard is a Florence-based writer, visual artist, art historian, speaker and landscape theorist. Two editions of *Blue Guide Northern Italy* have been published under his curatorship. He is also the author of *Blue Guide Southern Italy* and *Blue Guide Concise Italy*.

CONTENTS

PRACTICAL INFORMATION

ARRIVAL AND GETTING AROUND

LOCAL INFORMATION

ADDITIONAL INFORMATION

FOOD AND DRINK

MAPS

Introduction

Trentino-Alto Adige, the mountain territory of the upper Adige Valley and South Tyrol, incorporates the modern provinces of Bolzano and Trento. It is a semi-autonomous region: it has a special administrative order, much like that of the Valle d'Aosta, that reflects its multi-cultural (Germanic, Italian and Ladin) make-up. Most characteristic among the mountains of this region are the fantastic pinnacles of the Dolomites, the strangely shaped mountains disposed in irregular groups between the Adige and Pave valleys. Nine areas of this range, spread over five provinces, form a composite UNESCO World Heritage Site.

Strictly speaking, the Dolomites are a sub-range of the Eastern Alps. But anyone who has seen them knows that they are much more than that. 'The Dolomites... recall quaint Eastern architecture, whose daring pinnacles derive their charm from a studied defiance of the sober principles of stability.... The Dolomites are strange adventurous experiments, which one can scarcely believe to be formed of ordinary rock. They would have been fit background for the garden of Kublai Khan', wrote Leslie Stephen in *The Playground of Europe* (1871).

The province of Trento is almost entirely Italian speaking, with the notable exception of the Fassa valley north and east of Trento, where the Raeto-Romance language of Ladin is still spoken. In the province of Bolzano (the Alto Adige/South Tyrol) Ladin was, except in the more remote valleys, overlaid by German (the region was part of the Austro-Hungarian empire until 1918), then Italian; now Ladin, German and Italian are all recognized as official languages. The two provinces represent respectively the old ecclesiastic principalities of Trento and Bressanone (or Brixen), both of which in the Middle Ages paid nominal allegiance to the Holy Roman Empire. In the 14th and 15th centuries the bishop-princes held the balance between the rising power of Venice on the south and the Counts of Tyrol on the north, while in the 16th century, under the bishops Clesio of Trento and Madruzzo of Bressanone, the valleys were practically independent.

Local powers declined here as elsewhere in the 17th and 18th centuries, and the Trentino and southern Tyrol became more closely attached to the Holy Roman Empire. During Napoleon's campaigns the region was transferred from Austria to Bavaria; it was returned to Austria after the Congress of Vienna. Austrian misgovernment in the 19th century caused great discontent in the Trentino, and a movement for absorption into the Veneto was born. Following the collapse of the Austro-Hungarian Empire after the First World War, the Trentino came under Italian power, and the frontier was extended northward to the Brenner Pass.

Trento & The Trentino

T he gateway to the eastern Alps is the valley of the River Adige, the southern entrance to which is guarded by Trento and its sister city, Rovereto. To the east and west lies some of the finest country in the Italian Alps, including the soaring Adamello-Brenta group with the lovely Non and Sole valleys; and the peaks known as the Pale di San Martino, with the long, beautiful Val di Fiemme and Val di Fassa. There are marvellous parks in the high-mountain areas, and numerous summer and winter resorts in the valleys.

TRENTO

A cheerful provincial capital encircled by spectacular mountain ranges, Trento (*map A, B2–B3*) is the most liveable city in Italy, according to a 2013 survey. Though it remained in Austrian hands until 1918, it is a typically northern Italian city and entirely Italian speaking. It has a number of fine palaces and churches, a magnificent castle—the former seat of its bishop-princes—and a world-class science museum.

HISTORY OF TRENTO

A Raetian settlement, Trento was Romanised in the course of the 1st century BC and became a *municipium* and an honorary colony (called Tridentum) in the Antonine period. During the Middle Ages Trento owed its importance to its position on the main road from Germany to Italy. It became an episcopal fief in 1027, its bishops acquiring the temporal power that they held almost without interruption until 1802. Early in the 15th century the citizens rebelled against the overwhelming power of the bishops, but local unrest came to an end with the threat of a Venetian invasion, Venice having secured control of the Val Lagarina as far up as Rovereto (1416). The Tridentines (as the inhabitants of Trento are known) asked for help from the Count of Tyrol, the Venetians were defeated in 1487, and in 1511 Austria established a protectorate over the Trentino. In the 16th century the city rose to prominence under Bishop Bernardo Clesio and Bishop Cristoforo Madruzzo, and during the episcopate of the latter the famous Council of Trent (*see p. 9*) met here (1545–63). The last bishop-prince escaped from the French in 1796, and the Austrians took possession of the town in 1813, holding it until 1918 through a century of great unrest.

THE DUOMO AND ITS NEIGHBOURHOOD

Piazza del Duomo (*map Trento 5*) is the monumental centre of the city. It is an extraordinarily handsome square, with an 18th-century Neptune fountain standing in the shadow of the 13th-century Palazzo Pretorio and Torre Civica. Frescoes by Marcello Fogolino, court artist of bishop-prince Bernardo Clesio, adorn the Case Cazuffi, across the street.

On the south side of the square extends the austere left flank of the **cathedral of San Vigilio**, a Romanesque-Gothic building of the 12th and 13th centuries with a powerful 16th-century campanile and a Romanesque-revival dome. Faced entirely in marble, it has magnificent decorative detailing and a beautiful apse, against which stands the 13th-century Castelletto, with mullioned windows and a crenellated roof.

The cathedral interior has three tall aisles with compound piers, a small clerestory in the nave, and cross vaults. Arcaded staircases ascend the west wall, amid 16th-century tomb monuments, to the galleries. The large Cappella del Crocifisso, in the south aisle, preserves a 16th-century wooden crucifix, before which the decrees of the Council of Trent (*see box below*) were promulgated. In the transepts are remains of 13th- and 15th-century frescoes, and at the end of the north aisle, a 13th-century stone statue known as the *Madonna degli annegati* (*Madonna of the Drowned*), at the foot of which people drowned in the Adige were identified. The baldachin over the high altar is more or less a copy of that of St Peter's in Rome. Steps in the north transept lead down to the Early Christian basilica, which was rebuilt in the 11th century and replaced by the present building two centuries later. The remains include fragmentary mosaics, and sculptures.

Inside the Castelletto, clusters of tall columns carry the arcades, surmounted by a diminutive clerestory, and unusual arcaded staircases lead up to the galleries. It contains numerous tombs of bishops, 13th–14th-century frescoes (some attributed to Tommaso da Modena), a 13th-century statue of the Madonna, and two 13th-century marble reliefs of St Stephen.

The **Museo Diocesano** (*open Jun–Sept Mon, Wed, Thur and Fri 9.30–12.30 & 2.30–6; Sat and Sun 10–1 and 2–6; Oct–May Mon, Wed, Thur and Fri 9.30–12.30 & 2–5.30; Sat and Sun 10–1 & 2–6*) occupies the Palazzo Pretorio, once the bishops' palace. It has a wonderful and beautifully displayed collection of paintings and sculpture from local churches and the most valuable objects from the cathedral treasury. Highlights include a magnificent collection of wood sculptures, a fine series of 16th-century Flemish tapestries by Pieter van Aelst, and the 13th-century treasure of Bishop Federico Vanga.

Via Belenzani, an elegant shopping street, is flanked by Renaissance palaces showing a strong Venetian influence, some with painted façades. The best of these are the **Palazzo Geremia** (no. 20), with charming frescoes of the early 16th century showing the Emperor Maximilian, who stayed here in 1508–9, and members of his court; and Palazzo Alberti-Colico (no. 32). Across the street stands Palazzo Thun, today the Town Hall, with frescoes by Brusasorci in the Sala della Giunta. The new **Galleria Civica**, at Via Belenzani 44, presents changing exhibitions of art and architecture from the 19th century to the present (*open Tues–Sun 10–1 & 2–6*).

Vicolo Colico leads west from Via Belenzani to **Santa Maria Maggiore**, a

Renaissance church of 1520–4 with a remarkable doorway and a fine campanile. Several sessions of the Council of Trent were held here, including the last one. The great portal of the façade dates from 1535; on the south side is a 16th-century Lombardesque portal. The *Assumption* over the high altar is by Pietro Ricchi, a pupil of Guido Reni; the marble organ gallery of 1534 is a masterpiece of the Venetian sculptors Vincenzo and Gian Gerolamo Grandi.

Via Belenzani ends before the church of **San Francesco Saverio**, a fine example of local Baroque architecture; from here Via Manci and Via San Marco, its continuation, lead right past more 16th- and early-17th century houses, to the castle.

THE COUNCIL OF TRENT

The 19th Ecumenical Council of the Roman Catholic Church (1545–63) was convoked under Holy Roman Emperor Charles V in response to the spread of Protestantism across Europe. Alarmed by the number of Christians massing under Luther's banner, the emperor was concerned to put the Roman Catholic Church in order, addressing both church discipline and dogma. The council did not begin as a Counter Reformatory project to repudiate Protestants: Protestant delegates were present, and the original aim was to find a solution—this proved impossible. What the council concluded included the following: the Nicene Creed was the basis of faith; Luther, Calvin and Zwingli were all repudiated; the Catholic Church's stance on Original Sin, Transubstantiation, purgatory, indulgences, the veneration of relics and the role of the saints was defined. To the end the council was dogged by disagreement between pope and emperor. When Charles V died, his even less conciliatory brother Ferdinand succeeded him, and disagreement between the pope's prelates and those from Spain and the empire became worse than ever. In the end the papal faction prevailed. The Protestant question was not settled, but the Council's decrees formed a manual for Roman Catholicism that remained unchanged up to 1967.

THE CASTELLO DEL BUONCONSIGLIO

Once the stronghold of the bishop-princes of Trento, this imposing citadel (*map Trento 4; open Tues–Sun May–Oct 10–6, Nov–May 9.30–5*) is the largest and most important monumental complex of the Trentino-Alto Adige. The crenellated Castelvecchio on the north is the oldest part; it was built in the 13th century and altered in 1475. The Magno Palazzo on the south is a Renaissance edifice built in 1528–36 by Bernardo Clesio, then imperial chancellor, who intended it to express the power his position had brought him. Between the two rises the Giunta Albertina, a 17th-century addition built for bishop-prince Francesco Alberta Poja. The staircase and state rooms, bishop's apartments and library are known for their superb fresco decorations, dating mainly from the late Middle Ages to the Renaissance. They were painted by the central- and northern-Italian artists Dosso and Battista Dossi, Zaccaria Zacchi, Marcello Fogolino and Romanino, who are generally credited with bringing the Renaissance to Trento and its territory.

The Castello del Buonconsiglio is the chief of four castles recently restored and adapted to present the historical and artistic heritage of the Autonomous Province of Trento (the others are Castello di Stenico, in the Valla Giudicarie, Castel Beseno, in Valle dell'Adige between Trento and Rovereto, and Castel Thun, in the Valle di Non). The exhibits present the province's finest holdings of antiquities, medieval artworks, small bronzes and medals, codices, prints and drawings, coins, paintings and sculptures, as well as a unique collection of majolica stoves and tiles. The visit begins on the ground floor. Immediately beyond the entrance, rooms on the left and right are devoted, respectively, to **Egyptian antiquities** and **engraved stones**. The former were bequeathed by 19th- and early 20th-century collectors; the latter were collected after the mid-16th century by the bishop-prince Cristoforo Madruzzo, whose interest focused on antique epigraphs and marbles, and in the 19th century by mayor Benedetto Giovanelli, who added the stones from the Middle Ages and later periods.

Stairs frescoed by Marcello Fogolino with Renaissance decorative motifs and historical portraits (Charlemagne with dignitaries and soldiers, and the early bishops of Trento) lead up to the first-floor Loggia Veneziana, with Venetian-style trilobite arches. The **archaeology collection**, in the adjoining rooms, is the largest and most fascinating of the museum's holdings: on exhibit are more than six hundred objects representing the ancient populations of the region from prehistory, through Roman times to the early Middle Ages. The oldest were left by the nomadic hunters who were drawn to the area as they followed retreating glaciers northward in the Upper Palaeolithic period, around 11,000 BC. Metal objects from later epochs indicate the stabilisation of settlements and the growth of trade and social complexity. Particularly interesting are the exhibits regarding the Raetians—a term coined by the Romans to describe the peoples who inhabited the Alpine Arc from the 6th–1st centuries BC and whose civilisation shows northern Etruscan and Celtic influences. The Romanisation of the area is represented by artworks, jewellery and objects for daily use. Among the most unusual are the touching finds from the tomb of a well-to-do young girl, including her doll and jewels. With the disintegration of the Roman Empire, the Alpine Arc became a lawless borderland. Though it dwindled in size, Trento remained the seat of a powerful aristocracy, made up of Goths, Heruli, Byzantines and Lombards. The integration of these northern and eastern peoples into Roman society brought a reciprocal assimilation of customs that is reflected in the exhibits: weapons and jewellery—distinctive possessions of the upper social classes—mirror the traditions and innovations of a community that was by this time multi-ethnic.

The collections of **medieval art**, codices, drawings and prints, and coins and medals, are shown on a rotating basis throughout the castle. The medieval art holdings document the spread of Christianity, beginning with objects of daily use bearing Palaeochristian symbolic motifs, some 6th-century mosaics dedicated to Sts Cosmas and Damian, and the silver Sant'Apollinare reliquary, of the 6th or 7th century, found during a dig at the church of the same name. Here too are detached frescoes, sculptures, and a remarkable collection of ivory and bone domestic objects. The most dazzling codices are the 5th-century *Evangeliario Purpureo*, with purple-tinted pages and silver script, and the 9th-century *Sacramentario Gregoriano*, with an 8th-century ivory cover. The 15th-century musical and liturgical codices from the Feininger Collection, and the Trentino musical codices from the cathedral, are considered among the most valuable and important sources for the study of music in the early 15th century: some 2,000 sheets contain 1,864 mainly sacred polyphonic compositions by eighty-odd composers from England, France, Flanders and Italy.

More than 3,000 **drawings and prints** document the history of regional art, which includes outsiders working in the area as well as native artists. Among the several major legacies from private collectors, the most notable is the Lazzari Turco Menz collection of roughly 1,000 Italian, French, Flemish-Dutch, German, Spanish and English prints ranging from the 15th–19th centuries. The **numismatic collection** includes thousands of items—coins, medals, seals, plaques and more—ranging from antiquity to the Middle Ages, including some interesting 12th-century coins minted in Trento, Merano and Bressanone. The quantity and quality of the holdings makes the Castello del Buonconsiglio collection one of the most important anywhere.

The **painting collection** lines the walls of the Magna Palazzo and the Giunta Albertina. It ranges from the 15th–19th centuries and documents the region's artistic development with particular attention to native artists and artists from the Veneto and Lombardy who worked in the area. Of note among the 15th-century paintings are a *Madonna and Child* by a disciple of Stefano da Verona, and another by the Venetian artist Tommaso Bragadin. The 16th century, the highest moment in the history of Tridentine art, is represented by important regional artists such as Marcello Fogolino (altarpiece with the *Mystic Marriage of St Catherine*, with donors Andrea Borgo and Dorotea Thun), Altobello Melone (*Simonino*), Girolamo Romanino (*Madonna and Child with Saints*; *Visitation*, a fragmentary piece of the organ doors from the church of Santa Maria Maggiore), Jacob Seisenegger (*The Daughters of King Ferdinand I of Habsburg*) Giovanni Battista Moroni (*Annunciation*) and Paolo Farinati (an altarpiece commissioned by the Madruzzo family). The 17th century is represented by Pietro Ricchi, Alessandro Turchi, Francesco Maffei, Pietro Liberi, Carl Loth, Andrea Pozzo and the Flemish painter Giuseppe Alberti. The best 18th-century paintings are those of the so-called Fiemme School, by Michelangelo and Cristoforo Unterperger, and by Francesco Fontebasso and Giambettino Cignaroli. There is also a selection of paintings by the Neoclassical portraitist Giovanni Battista Lampi the Elder (1751–1830).

On the second floor, the **small bronzes and medals**, dating mainly from the Renaissance, are displayed in the Sala degli Specchi. Among the finest are the beautifully designed creations of Vicenzo and Gian Gerolamo Grandi of Padua: an example is the door-knocker made of two simple laurel branches in the form of a garland (1532–9). Here too are a delicate *Head of a Young Boy* attributed to Simone Bianco (c. 1525) and a small bronze *Venus Chastising Love* attributed to Nicola Roccatagliata (c. 1560–1636).

The wonderful collection of **wood sculptures** is located in the 16th-century Library of the bishop-prince. Here are works by artists representing both the Northern European and the Italian (mainly Lombard-Venetian) schools. The sculptures, ranging in date from the 14th to the 17th centuries, are arranged chronologically and by theme. Particularly fine are the small Romanesque Madonnas, among the oldest extant examples of local artistry, the elegant late-Gothic 'Beautiful Madonnas' showing Swabian and Bohemian influence, the moving *Annunciation* by the Brescia Maffeo Olivieri, the regal female figures of Jorge Atz and the captivating narrative reliefs by Narciso da Bolzano and his school.

The visit ends with the museum's unusual collection of **stoves and majolica tiles**, on the third floor of the Castelvecchio. The stove is among the most valuable furnishings in traditional alpine interiors, and in the past its decoration was often very refined. Displayed here are a number of works made in the Trentino and South Tyrol from the Renaissance to the 18th century.

A custodian takes groups of visitors into the **towers** to see their exceptionally delicate frescoed rooms and a part of the old fortifications. Normally, groups depart at 20-min intervals and the visit costs an additional euro (for the obligatory audio guide), but is well worth it. On a commission from Clesio the **Torre del Falcon** was decorated after 1530 by an anonymous German painter, with a delightful series of hunting scenes; the city in the background is Salzburg, Austria. In the **Torre dell'Aquila** are the castle's most famous frescoes, commissioned probably from a Bohemian artist by bishop-prince Giorgio di Liechtenstein, around 1400. Known as the *Cycle of the Months*, they are a perfect compendium of farming in the South Tyrol. In eleven handsome frames (March, unfortunately, has been destroyed) they show seasonal agricultural activities in the minutest detail. Harvests are plentiful and life is good—especially for some: in winter while the peasants prepare for the spring planting, the nobles frolic in the snow.

The castle complex also houses the **Museo Civico del Risorgimento e della Lotta per la Liberazione** (*open as the Museo del Castello*) with memorabilia mainly of the Irredentist movement, of the First World War and of the Resistance.

ALONG THE RIVER

Trento's newest and finest museum, **MUSE—Muse delle Scienze di Trento** (*map Trento 7*) is the centrepiece of the newly redeveloped Albere industrial district. The new neighbourhood, ten minutes south of the cathedral, on foot, also includes very attractive residential and retail spaces and a large park with playgrounds. The district, largely powered by solar energy and heated and cooled by heat pumps, meets the highest European (Klimahaus) and American (Energy Star) standards of sustainability.

The spectacular science museum (*open Tues–Fri 10–6; Sat, Sun and holidays 10–7*) was designed by Renzo Piano and inaugurated in July 2013. It develops on five floors above ground and one below, around a large central well populated by alpine birds and mammals suspended in space on thin steel cables. The curatorial project uses a mountain metaphor to tell of life on Earth. The visit begins at the top—on the fourth floor and the rooftop terrace—then descends to explore the themes of life at high altitudes, biodiversity, sustainability and evolution, ending in the luxuriant basement-level greenhouse. The fourth floor is dedicated to high-elevation environments; highlights here are the full-surround digital simulation of an avalanche, and a hands-on *via ferrata* (a hiking trail equipped with fixed cables one can harness oneself to for safety, invented by the Italian military in World War I to allow troops to reach inaccessible mountain positions) suspended at the edge of the 23-metre deep central well. The first-floor displays trace the history of human presence in the Alps, illustrating human cultural, economic and social evolution from Neanderthal man, through the arrival of *Homo sapiens*, to the Stone Age and the Age of Metals. Highlights include rock paintings of plants and animals from the Riparo Dalmeri, a large open cave on the northern rim of the Piana della Marcèsina (1200m).

The basement-level 'Traces of Life' displays provide a general account of the development of life on earth, with specific insights into key issues such as the nature and character of DNA.

Across the park from MUSE is **Palazzo delle Albere**, a formerly suburban villa encircled by a moat, built around 1535 for bishop-prince Cristoforo Madruzzo. Decorated with frescoes of which only traces remain today, it is home to the 19th-century and early Modern section of **MART, the Museo d'Arte Moderna e Contemporanea di Rovereto e Trento**, presenting artworks made before 1918 and temporary exhibitions (*closed for restoration at the time of writing*).

MUSEO AERONAUTICO GIANNI CAPRONI

This museum (*open Tues–Fri 10–1 & 2–6; Sat, Sun and holidays 10–6*), at Mattarello, near the airport (*shuttle bus from MUSE at weekends*), was founded in 1927 by aviation pioneer Gianni Caproni, a native of Arco, and his wife Timina Guasti. It is the oldest aviation museum in the world. Here you'll find an exceptional collection of historical aircraft, together with other material documents of humankind's conquest of the air—machinery, prints, drawings, photographs, archival documents, books and artworks—all assembled over the years by the Caproni family. The focus is on the early years of flight, and nine of the historical aircraft are the only extant examples of their kind.

GIANNI CAPRONI

A graduate of the famous University of Technology in Munich, Caproni designed his first aeroplane after witnessing a demonstration flight by the Wright Brothers. In 1910 he founded the first of several firms that would bear his name, test-flying his prototype (the Ca.1) in June of that year. He was one of the first aviation engineers to develop monoplanes (in 1911: Ca.8–Ca.16), and the first to produce an aircraft specifically designed to carry bombs (Ca.31, used in the First World War by the French and Italians under the name Ca.1–3). After the Great War he shifted the firm's focus to civil aviation, developing the first prototype for a long-range airliner, the Caproni Ca.60 *Transaereo*, a giant flying boat for 100 passengers intended for Transatlantic routes. With the advent of Fascism the focus returned to military aircraft, in which field the firm attained further distinction with the Caproni Ca.73 night bomber, the largest land-based aircraft in the world from 1929 to 1934. By the mid-30s the Caproni Group had become a multinational, with affiliates in Europe and the United States (Caproni-Curtiss). Caproni aircraft at this time broke all world distance, altitude and speed records, including the highest flight by a woman (Carina Negrone, 12,043m, 20 June 1935 in a Ca.113). A vigorous opponent of Italy's entry into World War II, Caproni rightly predicted that it would be a war of machines to be won by the side that deployed the best in the largest numbers; not surprisingly, the Caproni Group provided the Italian Royal Air Force with fighters, bombers and reconnaissance planes throughout the conflict. Tried and acquitted of favouring the Fascist regime, immediately after the war, Caproni attempted but failed to recapitalise the firm, which shut down in the early 50s. He died in 1957.

The collection is displayed in two hangars and on the airport apron in summer. In addition to Caproni aircraft and engines it includes planes made by other manufactures (notably the Macchi M20, 1918–20, possibly the most charming aeroplane ever built), interactive multimedia displays, and a full-scale simulator of the Ansaldo SVA (the fastest Allied combat aircraft in World War I, chosen by Gabriele d'Annunzio for the famous Flight Over Vienna of 9th August 1918) where the only thing lacking is the wind in your hair.

ENVIRONS OF TRENTO

Monte Bondone, cloaked in forests, overlooks the city from the southwest. It is known for its alpine flora (it produces herbs used in baths in special establishments) and as a ski resort. The Conca delle Viotte, a glacial depression set beneath the peaks of the massif (Palon, 2090m; Doss d'Abramo, 2140m; Monte Cornetto, 2180m) hosts the **Giardino Botanic Alpino** (*open June and Sept 9–5, July and Aug 9–6*), with over a thousand plant species from the Trentino and the principal mountains of the world, particularly medicinal plants threatened by extinction. The garden is part of the Riserva Naturale delle Tre Cime del Monte Bondone, which also includes an 'integral' nature reserve accessible only to researchers.

Castel Beseno (*open Nov–March Sat–Sun 9.30–5, March–May Tues–Sun 9.30–5, May–Nov Tues–Sun 10–6*) which controlled the valley south of Trento, rises above Calliano on the way to Rovereto. The hill was inhabited in the Iron Age, as well as in the Roman and Lombard periods. The castle dates from the 12th century and was owned by the Castelbarco from 1303 until the 15th century, when it was given to the Trapp family, who donated it to the province in 1973. It has recently been restored to host temporary exhibitions and includes two large courtyards within its impressive walls. A room of the castle preserves 16t- century frescoes of the Months.

There are several beautiful lakes around Trento. The **Lago di Toblino** (*map A, B3*), lying amid rocky mountains in the valley of the Sacra, 16km west of the city, is overlooked by a medieval castle. The lake is separated by an isthmus from the **Lago di Santa Massenza**, surrounded by olive trees. Roughly 20km east of the city in the Valsugana are the picturesque Lago di Caldonazzo and Lago di Levico, the latter with a thermal resort, **Levico Terme** (*map A, C3*).

WHERE TO STAY IN AND AROUND TRENTO

Fai della Paganella (*map A, B2*)
€ **Florandonole**. Fai della Paganella is a quiet village (with a panoramic nature trail) a short drive north from Trento's Monte Bondone ski slopes. Florandonole stands on its outskirts, amidst meadows and at the edge of larch and fir forests. Here Andrea and Lucia have created one of the most unusual *agriturismi* in the Trentino. Their new house is built in a contemporary vernacular style, with a cultivated but unpretentious use of natural wood, glass, stone and white plaster. The rooms are warm and comfortable, and some can be connected to form suites. Lucia's 'farmhouse dinners', prepared for guests at weekends, would drive the most severe food critic to ecstasy: if this is how the farmers eat, imagine the lords of the land... Andrea and Lucia are also beekeepers, producing delicious honeys. About a dozen different varieties, from super-sweet rhododendron, through aromatic dandelion-apple blossom, to bittersweet chestnut. You can also order it online. *Via Carmelo 18a, T: 0461 581039, http://florandonole.it/.*

Levico Terme (*map A, C3*)
€€€ **Imperial Grand Hotel Terme**. This magnificent villa, set like a jewel in a luxuriant park of 150,000m², was built as a summer residence of the Austrian imperial family. 'Splendour' and 'refine-ment' are the first words that come to mind, but 'restraint' is not far behind: the lobby, dining room and other public areas are in fact quite sober, their elegance deriving from understatement. The same quiet sophistication characterises most of the rooms. There are an indoor restaurant and an outdoor grill by the pool, both offering light, delicious dishes based on the finest locally sourced ingredients. The main attraction of course is the spa, where you can soothe your body in the thermal waters or indulge in any number of health and beauty treatments. The staff is experienced and very courteous. *Via Silva Domini 1. T: 0461 706104, www. imperialhotel.it.*

Trento (*map A, B3*)
€ **B&B Al Cavour 34**. In the historic Palazzo Gallo in the heart of Trento, around the corner from the duomo and a five-minute walk from the station, this tiny bed and breakfast (just three rooms) opened its doors at the end of 2013. The young hosts earned their spurs in the luxury hotel business, and their experience shows, both in the quality of the accommodation and in the style of management—which together with the tasteful, discreet renovation places this B&B firmly among the best values in the region. *Via Camillo Benso Cavour 34, T: 349 415 5814. Map Trento, 5.*

WHERE TO EAT IN AND AROUND TRENTO

PERGINE VALSUGANA (*map A, B3–C3*)
€€ **Castel Pergine**. This excellent country restaurant, occupying historic rooms in a 10th-century castle, is one of the few places in the Trentino serving delicious vegetarian and vegan meals—not dishes, complete meals. It comes attached to a small hotel; the sober but comfortable rooms are in the 16th-century wing built for the Council of Trent,

and in the towers. The castle is set on a knoll enjoying marvellous views over the surrounding countryside. It is a venue for exhibitions of contemporary art in summer. *Via al Castello 10, T: 0461 531158, www.castelpergine.it.*

TRENTO (*map A, B3*)

€€ **Antica Trattoria Due Mori**. In the historic city centre a stone's throw from the Castello del Buonconsiglio, this historic restaurant provides very good value and wonderful atmosphere. The food is straightforward and unpretentious mountain fare, and the excellent wines are reasonably priced. NB: portions can be quite large. *Via San Marco 11, T: 0461 984251, www.ristoranteduemori.com. Map Trento, 6.*

€€ **Le Due Spade**. This fine old *osteria*, just a few paces from the duomo (and with summer seating outside enjoying great views of the west front) was established in 1545 to serve the clerics attending the Council of Trent. It offers delicious creative interpretations of traditional recipes, accompanied by regional, Italian and imported wines. Among the rooms is a historic wood-panelled *Stube* with great green majolica stove. *Via Don Rizzi 11, T: 0461 234343, www.leduespade.com. Map Trento, 5.*

€€ **Scrigno del Duomo**. This bistro-style restaurant and wine bar enjoys a fabulous location on the west side of Piazza Duomo, and the menu and wine list are as beautiful, in their way, as the square itself. The building dates from the Middle Ages; frescoes by an unknown Renaissance artist adorn the façade, and the attractive 15th-century interior has magnificent painted-wood ceilings and fragments of a Roman wall. Small works by contemporary artists hang in the dining rooms. Everything is delicious and well-presented; the picture would be perfect were it not for the service, which when the restaurant is crowded (reservations are not taken) can be excruciatingly slow. There is seating in the little forecourt in summer. *Piazza Duomo 29, T: 0461 220030, www.scrignodelduomo.com. Map Trento, 5.*

€ **Maso Finisterre.**

You'll need a car (or a taxi) to reach this fantastic country restaurant in a renovated farmhouse on Trento's southern outskirts. Especially in summer, when meals are served in the garden, it's one of the most pleasant (and satisfying) places in town. Recorded in the 18th century as a property of the Counts of Thun, the Maso Finistrerre is still the heart of a working farm. The restaurant has served delicious country cooking since 2009, focusing on traditional dishes such as *strangolapreti* and *strigoli* with speck and woodruff, roast goat and wines and cheeses from the surrounding hills. *Via Santi Cosma e Damiano 6, T: 0461 825752, www.ristorantemasofinisterre.com. Beyond map Trento, 1.*

Rovereto & its Environs

Rovereto (*map A, B3*), a city possibly of Roman origin, spreads out at the foot of its 14th-century castle. Behind the historic façades of Corso Bettini, the main street of the old town centre, lies one of the jewels of modern culture in Northern Italy, the **MART–Muse d'Arte Moderna e Contemporanea di Rovereto e Trento** (*open Tues–Thur 10–6, Fri 10–9, Sat and Sun 10–8*). The museum exhibits the finest collection of Italian Modernism anywhere: works by Fortunato Depero (a native of Rovereto), Filippo Tommaso Marinetti, Giacomo Balla, Encrico Prampolini and other artists of the Futurist area, are displayed together with paintings and sculptures by artists ranging in date from the early years of the 20th century until the present day (Fontana, Burri, Merz and others) as well as significant works of European and American contemporary art. The museum also mounts important temporary exhibitions, including exhibitions of old masters.

FAST, FURIOUS FUTURISM

The Futurist movement was launched by a manifesto, published on 20th February 1909 on the front page of the Paris newspaper *Le Figaro*, and written by the Italian poet and playwright Filippo Tommaso Marinetti. In ringing, romantic tones Marinetti hailed the new world of mechanical forces and denounced all attachment to the past. He glorified speed and aggression, patriotism and war, and he promised to destroy museums and libraries as reliquaries of the past. Among all the rhetoric, the words that were remembered most readily were those he used to exemplify that 'new form of beauty, the beauty of speed': 'A racing car, its hood adorned with pipes like serpents with explosive breath...a racing car that seems to run on gunpowder is more beautiful than the *Victory of Samothrace*'. Thus he put into memorable opposition an industrial product, created to unprecedented standards of efficiency and power, with a work of art created in emulation of an established standard of beauty, the famous Hellenistic sculpture admired by visitors to the Louvre.

The painters Umberto Boccioni, Carlo Carrà, Luigi Russolo, Giacomo Balla and Gino Severini publicly proclaimed their adherence to the movement in March 1910, following this a month later with a technical manifesto of Futurist painting. Boccioni published a manifesto of Futurist culture in 1912, and a Futurist exhibition in Paris in 1912 was accompanied by a further manifesto defining the theoretic bases of the movement. Antonio Sant'Elia penned the manifesto of Futurist architecture in 1914.

Fortunato Depero joined the movement that same year, co-authoring, with Umberto Boccioni, the manifesto *Futurist Reconstruction of the Universe*, which called for a blending of artistic media and greater interaction between art and life, in 1915

Futurism did not endeavour to reconstruct reality or to express individuality (as Cubism and Expressionism did). It tried to embrace—in a naïve, exalted and somewhat provincial way—the world of the machine, speed and progress. Even with these limits, one must admit the merits of Futurism, which consisted essentially in recognising, for the first time in a radical way, the inadequacy of traditional artistic languages and the necessity of breaking free of fossilised culture. The Futurists' ideas, in literature and in the arts, turned out to be ephemeral and largely impracticable, and in fact were soon abandoned. But in the mean time Italy had gone through a state of intense experimentation, the consequences of which would not soon be forgotten. In Russia, its effect was felt both by the Rayonists and by Vladimir Tatlin, a seminal figure in Russian Constructivism. The Dadaists owned something to it, particularly in their noisy publicity techniques, and in England it had considerable effect on Vorticism and C.R.W. Nevinson. In France Marcel Duchamp and Robert Delaunay, among others, developed the Futurist ideas about the representation of movement in their own ways.

Fortunato Depero's **Casa d'Arte Futurista**, in the heart of the old town (*Via dei Portici 38, open Tues–Sun 10–6*), is one of the earliest manifestations of Modernism's aspiration to break down the barriers between the 'high culture' of art and the practical needs of everyday life. Depero himself conceived the Casa d'Arte—the only museum founded by a Futurist—not only to display the tapestries, furniture, toys and other objects he himself designed, but also as a workshop and research laboratory where others might develop their ideas—an aspiration that has now found public support. Architect Renate Rizzi's 2009 renovation is one of the finest examples in Italy of the integration of contemporary and traditional architectural values.

Nearby, the 15th-century **Palazzo del Municipio** has remains of façade frescoes attributed to Fogolino, and the contemporary Palazzo della Cassa di Risparmio shows Venetian influence. The **Museo Civico** (*Borgo Santa Caterina 41, open Tues–Sun 9–12 & 3–6; July–Oct Fri and Sun also 8–10pm*), first opened to the public in 1855, houses the collections of the archaeologist Paolo Orsi (1849–1925), who was a native of the town, as well as a planetarium and a natural history section.

Rovereto's castle is now home to the **Museo Storico Italiano della Guerra** (*open July–Sept Tues–Fri 10–6, Sat and Sun 10–7; Oct–May Tues–Fri 10–6*), with some 30 rooms devoted to the First World War and a section devoted to the Napoleonic wars, 19th-century arms and armies and the Italian Risorgimento. The Great War is commemorated also by the Sacrario (1936) and the Campana dei Caduti, the largest bell in Italy, which tolls every evening for the fallen of all nations. The front line of 1916–18 was in the mountains south of the town.

At **Monte Zugna** (20km south of Rovereto), a joint project undertaken by the

Museo Storico Italiano della Guerra in cooperation with the Museo Civico and the Fondazione Parco Botanico del Cengio Alto di Rovereto, has recovered some impressive First World War artefacts in the area of the Trincerone/Kopfstellung. The restoration of the first Italian and Austro-Hungarian lines, coordinated by architects Alessandro Andreolli and Giorgio Campolongo, has created an educational walk around and through the trenches; text panels explain the military organisation of the mountain and offer details on the individual artefacts. The project, completed in 2011, was awarded the Costruire il Trentino prize for contemporary architecture in 2013.

WHERE TO STAY IN AND AROUND ROVERETO

NOGAREDO (*map A, B3*)

€ Relais Palazzo Lodron. This historic house was begun in the 15th century and finished in the 17th by the Nogoredo-born bishop-prince of Salzburg, Paris von Lodron. The architect was Santino Solari (1576–1646), who also worked on Salzburg cathedral and designed the city's Italian Baroque castle, Hellbrunn. The relais is a thoroughly comfortable place where antiques and designer furniture, old paintings and the odd piece of contemporary art stand side by side. The individually furnished rooms and suites are large and well-appointed, some with period furniture, others in a restrained contemporary style. Spa facilities include an indoor pool, Finnish sauna and cooler bio sauna (with aromatic herbs). Breakfast is served in the handsome garden in summer. *Via Conti Lodron 5, T: 0464 413152, http://www. relaispalazzolodron.it.*

The Adamello-Brenta Mountains

The west flank of the Adige Valley, opposite Trento, is formed by the Presanella and Brenta mountain groups, which, together with the east flank of Monte Adamello (3539m), constitute a protected area rich in sights of natural and historic interest.

In the Valla Giudicarie, between Stenico and Tione, is the **Gola della Scaletta**, a narrow winding gorge of the Sacra. **Stenico castle** (*map A, A3; open Nov–May Tues–Sun 9.30–5; May–Nov Tues–Sun 10–6*), dating from the 12th century, was the summer residence of the bishop-princes of Trento. It is now one of the four principal fine-arts museums of the Autonomous Province of Trento. The chapel bears Romanesque frescoes of New Testament scenes and saints (13th century); the rooms are frescoed with historical scenes, floral motifs and heraldic emblems, battle scenes and allegorical figures. The museum displays landscape, religious and portrait paintings; fine furniture; objects of daily use (including some very beautiful majolica stoves); antiquities from regional excavations and a very particular and fascinating collection of bells.

A winding road leads north from Stenico to the lovely, peaceful **Lago di Molveno**, 6.5km long, lying under the lee of the Brenta mountains. Spectacular walks can be taken in the area.

The lovely **Val di Non**—the ancient Ansonia—with its woods and ruined castles, is known for its apples: the landscape is particularly beautiful in spring when the trees are in blossom. A scenic branch railway line runs through the valley, connecting Trento to Malè. The most important place along the way is **Cles** (*map A, B1*), whose castle, the ancestral home of the famous episcopal Clesio family, was rebuilt in the 16th century. Standing at the foot of Monte Peller (2319m), the northern peak of the Brenta group, the town has a good Renaissance church and old houses. Cles spreads over a small rise overlooking the beautiful Lago di Santa Giustina; 20km south is the little **Lago di Tovel**, even prettier.

Also pleasant is **Sanzeno** (*map A, B1*), a village with a large 15th-century church built on the site of the martyrdom in 397 of the early Christian evangelisers Sisinius, Martyrius and Alexander from Cappadocia. The hills around Sanzeno have been inhabited since the Stone Age, and the new **Museo Retico** (*Via Nazionale 50, open late June–late Sept Tues–Sun 10–6; late Sept–Nov and March–late June Sat, Sun* *and holidays 2–6*) holds a fascinating collection of archaeological finds ranging from prehistory to the early Middle Ages. Here you can see the material culture of Palaeolithic hunter-gatherers, the first Neolithic farmers and breeders, the metal-workers of the Copper Age (represented also by some beautifully carved standing stones), as well as cult objects from Bronze-Age religious sanctuaries. There is a wide range of material relating to Raetic culture (with Fritzen, in Austria, Sanzeno gives its name to the late Iron-Age Fritzen-Sanzeno Culture, the culture most represent-ative of the pre-Roman inhabitants of the Alps), including statues, religious objects, tools and utensils, and simple everyday objects. Romanisation of the region is repre-sented by sculpture, burial artefacts, inscriptions and religious objects document-ing the arrival of new cults from the East—not the least of which, Christianity—as well as the story of the Martyrs of Aunonia. The installation, which makes unusually imaginative use of Sergio Giovanazzi's Deconstructivist architectural envelope, was created by the famous exhibition designer Maurizio Buffa of Turin. A nature trail ascends from the museum to the sanctuary of **San Romedio**, a pilgrim shrine on a steep rock above the village.

Castel Thun, overlooking the Val di Non from a knoll above Vigo di Ton, was the seat of one the most important noble families of the region. The castle (*open May–Nov Tues–Sun 10–6; Nov–March Sat and Sun 9.30–5; April–May Tues–Sun 9.30–5*) is a rare example of an aristocratic residence whose original furniture and exceptional art collection, assembled by the family over many centuries, has sur-vived intact. The complex system of fortifications, with its towers, walls, bastions, parapets and trenches, owes its present appearance to a 16th-century renovation. Inside, the walls are hung with family portraits, landscapes, still lifes, and reli-gious and mythological paintings by Jacopo Bassano, Camillo Procaccini, Giuseppe Maria Crispi, Giovanni Battista Lampe and Joseph Berger, among others. The most impressive of the many rooms is probably the 16th-century Stanza del Vescovo, whose walls are lined with beautiful stone-pine panelling.

To the northwest of Cles is the **Val di Sole**, the upper glen of the Noce (now used for canoeing and rafting). **Malè** (*map A, B1*), the main village in the valley, has a local ethnographical museum (Museo della Civiltà Solandra).

Madonna di Campiglio (1522m; *map A, A2*) is a famous winter and summer resort in a wooded basin in the upper valley of the Sacra, below the Brenta moun-tains. It has excellent ski facilities. The Brenta peaks, an isolated dolomitic group between Madonna di Campiglio and the Adige valley, are for expert climbers only, but there are many easier walks (marked by coloured signs) in their foothills. A path (or chair-lift) ascends Monte Spinal (2104m), from which there is a splendid circu-lar view of the Brenta, Adamello, Presanella and Ortler mountains. To the south is the magnificent **Val Brenta**.

Pinzolo (*map A, A2*), another ski resort and climbing centre, is in a splendid posi-tion at the junction of the two main upper valleys of the Sarca. The church of San Vigilio has a remarkable external fresco of the *Dance of Death* by Simone Baschenis (1539). A similar painting (1519) by the same artist decorates the exterior of the church of Santo Stefano, which also contains frescoes by him inside.

The **Val di Genova** is a magnificent valley, thickly wooded in parts and with several waterfalls, which is the main approach to the Presanella and Adamello groups from the east. The Presanella (3556m) was first ascended by the English alpinist Douglas Freshfield (d. 1929) in 1864.

THE ADAMELLO-BRENTA NATURE RESERVE

Park offices: Strembo (Val Rendena), Via Nazionale 12, T: 0465 804637.
Visitor centres (with themed displays): Daone, Casa della Fauna–Villa De
Bias, T: 0465 674989; Tuenno (Val di Non), Casa del Lago Rosso, T: 0463
451033; Spormaggiore, Casa dell'Orso, T: 0461 653622; Stenico, Casa della
Flora, T: 0465 702579; San Lorenzo in Banal, Casa c'era una volta, T: 0465
734040. www.pnab.it.

The largest protected area in the Trentino, the Adamello-Brenta Nature Reserve extends from the Dolomiti di Brenta on the east to the Adamello and Presanella massifs on the west. It forms a sort of natural bridge between the limestone-like Dolomites and the granite massifs of the Central Alps, presenting visitors with majestic glaciers, secluded high-mountain lakes and a variety of flora and fauna.

The flora of the reserve reads like an encyclopaedia of southern alpine plant life, with splendid forests—consisting mainly of red and white firs, larches and Scots pines at higher altitudes, and oaks, maples, sorbs, hazels, alders and cornels below—growing to an altitude of c. 2000m—and colonies of mugo pine, dwarf willow and rhododendron reaching to 2500m. As elsewhere in the Alps, thousands of years of human presence have left their mark: not only is settlement intense in valley areas, seasonal grazing has reduced the extent of the autochthonous high-altitude plants, turning many of the areas above the tree line into pasture. These high meadows have, in their turn, been colonised by innumerable species of Alpine wildflowers— notably gentians, anemones, arnicas, Alpine poppies, edelweiss and several kinds of lily.

The reserve is the last refuge in Italy of the Alpine brown bear, who shares the woodlands with numerous chamois, roe deer, marmots and rare birds. As a rule the bear are too few and too secluded (they live largely on the wild northeast slopes of the Brenta) to be sighted, but chamois are quite common: there were over 6000 at last count, nearly half the population of the Trentino. They and the park's 5000 deer can best be seen at dawn and dusk. Marmots abound above the tree line, and squirrel, weasel, hare and other small animals fill the forests. Birdlife includes white partridge, wood grouse, woodpeckers, owls, cuckoos, hawks and eagles.

WHERE TO STAY IN THE ADAMELLO-BRENTA

PINZOLO (*map A, A2*)
€€ Maso Doss. With just six rooms in an ancient 17th-century farmhouse, away from the crowds, this is a perfect place for those who love the great outdoors plus good food and wine. The rooms, small and cosy, are furnished in the same warm rustic style that characterises the kitchen and dining area. This was a one-room cabin when Ugo and Mariuccia Caola bought it in the 1970s. After fixing it up they started having friends over, and only accidentally began renting rooms to passers-by. You still feel as if you're with family here: guests all dine around two big tables, and the isolation of the place makes it easy to form friendships—even if your Italian is less than perfect. *Via Brenta 72, Sant'Antonio di Mavignolat, T: 0465 502758, www. masodoss.com.*

REVÒ (*map A, B1*)
€ B&B Casa Incantata. Set among apple orchards on the outskirts of a small village in the Val di Non, this attractive B&B was created by renovating a dull, anonymous house from the 1970s. The existing building was demolished and a new, much simpler building was built, preserving the original proportions and volumes and drawing on the essential traits of traditional alpine architecture: a compact, monolithic body, white plaster and exterior finishings, and natural wood-framed doors and windows. The only exceptions to the local vernacular are the containment of the gutters within the perimeter walls and the free scattering of doors and windows, which flood the interior with warm, natural light and offer marvellous views of the valley and its lake. The building is rated A+ by Klimahaus, an independent rating agency, for its use of innovative, environmentally friendly energy management techniques. Architecture by Paolo De Benedictis and Glenda Flaim (Venice), 2012. *Via Conti Arsio 19, T: 0463 432152, www.casaincantata.it.*

WHERE TO EAT IN THE ADAMELLO-BRENTA

MALÈ (*map A, B1*)
€€ CONTE RAMPONI. Expect excellent traditional fare and atmosphere to match in this locally popular restaurant in a 16th-century building. Low-vaulted ceilings, wood panelling and a great old ceramic stove ideally complement the hearty mountain cuisine. *Piazza San Marco 38, Magras, T: 0463 901989.*

The Val di Fiemme & Val di Fassa

Cavalese (*map A, C2*) is the main village in the Val di Fiemme, northeast of Trento. Like many of the valleys of the Pyrenees, this glen has preserved something of its medieval independence, and the 'Magnificent Comunità', installed in the ancient palace of the bishops of Trento, still administers the valuable communal lands. The palace contains a museum (*open Tues–Sun 3–7*) illustrating the history of the valley and containing 150 works by the Fiemme School of 17th-century painters.

The Ladin-speaking Val di Fassa is in the heart of the Dolomites; between Pozza di Fassa and Canazei it forms part of the Strada dei Dolomiti. The main village is **Vigo di Fassa/Vich de Fascia** (1382m; *map A, D1*), a winter sports resort. The new Museo Ladino here (Località San Giovanni/Sèn Jan, *open June–Sept and late Dec–early Jan, daily 10–12.30 & 3–5; closed Nov and early June; other periods Tues–Sat 3–7*) was designed by Ettore Sottsass, a pillar of 20th-century Italian design, who was of Ladin descent. Here are housed the ethnographic collections of the prestigious Istitut Cultural Ladin, which invested 20 years of research in their construction. The exhibits trace the development of the Ladin people through their material and spiritual culture, from prehistory to the present, focusing particularly on institutional organization, civic and religious values and traditions, the advent of mass tourism and alpinism. The mountains that rise above Vigo, the fantastic **Torri del Vaiolet**, are among the most dramatic peaks of the Dolomites.

THE PANEVEGGIO-PALE DI SAN MARTINO NATURE RESERVE

Park offices: Tonadico, Via Roma 19, T: 0439 64854; Visitor centres: Predazzo, Strada Statale per il Rolle, Località Paneveggio, T: 0462 576283; San Martino di Castrozza, Via Laghetto, 0439 768859; Tonadico, Via Castelpietra 2, Località Val Canali, T: 0439 64854. www.parks.it/parco.paneveggio. pale.s.martino/Eindex.php.

The marvellous peaks of the Pale di San Martino (3192m) and the vast national forest of Paneveggio, to the east of Predazzo, comprise the most spectacular nature reserve in the province of Trento. It is an area of extraordinary beauty, marred only by the presence of ski slopes around the popular resort of San Martino di Castrozza.

The great green mantle of the **Foresta di Paneveggio**, which occupies the upper valley of the Travignolo, includes 2690 hectares of conifers and 1300 hectares of active pastures. Although it suffered extensive damage during the First World War, it remains an example (rare in Italy) of correct forest management, where a century-old tradition, inaugurated during the Austro-Hungarian period, has been carefully preserved. Here you'll find red and white firs, larches, cembra pines, yews and various deciduous trees, including beeches, oaks and aspens. At higher altitudes the ground is covered with scrub pine and rhododendron, whortleberry and heather. The best area for flowers is the Val Venegia, where you can find rare endemisms such as *Saxifraga facchinii, Primula tyrolensis*, the arctic rush *Juncus arcticus* and the flecked marsh orchid *Dactilorhiza cruenta*.

The park's fauna includes hundreds of chamois and roe deer. Also present in good numbers are marmot, squirrel, hare, ermine, weasel, marten and fox. Among the more interesting birds are the royal eagle, dwarf owl, white partridge and black woodpecker.

WHERE TO STAY AND EAT IN THE VAL DI FIEMME AND VAL DI FASSA

REDAGNO/RADEIN

€€ Zirmerhof. Idyllically located at 1560m above sea level, Zirmerhof embodies the Perwanger family's own particular tradition of alpine hospitality, which dates back to 1890 when a small guest house was established here, and has become more refined over the decades. Rural history is everywhere: in the beams and vaults, in the Tyrolean *Stube*, in the library and throughout the public rooms, with their fireplaces and traditional tiled stoves. Authentic wood panelling, antiques and paintings abound, and there are murals in the dining room. The kitchen and wine cellar exceed expectations. Peaceful and romantic, the Zirmer also offers unparalleled views in all directions and an endless variety of walks. *Redagno di Sopra (southeast of Aldino; map A, C1), T: 0471 887215, www.zirmerhof.com*.

SORAGA (*map A, D1*)

€ Fuciade. In Ladin a *fuciade* is a haymeadow. This one is set at an elevation of roughly 2000m, with stunning views over mountains, meadows and forests. The Rifugio Fuciade, an alpine hut (with rooms) is known throughout the Val di Fassa for its for exquisite traditional food. The house itself is a recent construction but the hamlet is a thousand years old, and proprietor and chef Sergio Rossi is an authority on Ladin cuisine. The hut is accessible on foot in summer (45mins, moderate) or on skis or snow cat in winter (telephone ahead to reserve a ride). *Località Fuciade (Passo di San Pellegrino), T: 0462 574281, www.fuciade.it*.

TESERO

€ Artemisia. This working farm in the Val di Fiemme (just north of Panchia; *map A, C2*) offers accommodation in a serene contemporary house, heated and powered exclusively by renewable energy sources. Here you can enjoy world-class cross-country skiing (100km of trails) or long summer hikes in the silence of meadows and forests. There are just four tastefully decorated rooms, and accommodation is B&B, though guests are welcome to use the beautiful common kitchen. *Via Cerin 6, T: 0462 810210, www.agriturartemisia. it.*

Bolzano & the Alto Adige (South Tyrol)

T o the east of the provincial capital of Bolzano rise the pale rock towers of the Dolomites; to the west the dark grey granite peaks of the Central Alps. The difference in atmosphere between the two areas is remarkable. The Dolomites are more picturesque; the Central Alps are higher and more imposing, and covered with snow much of the year. There are magnificent nature reserves in both areas—the most accessible, the Riserva Naturale Sciliar-Catinaccio, is just a stone's throw from Bolzano—and summer and winter resorts abound.

BOLZANO

Bolzano, in German Bozen (*map B, B2*), is the largest town in the upper basin of the Adige and has been the capital of the (mainly German-speaking) province of Bolzano (known also as Alto Adige or South Tyrol) since 1927. It has the character of a German rather than an Italian town, although its population is now mainly Italian-speaking. The old town, with its low-pitched Tyrolean arcades and Gothic architecture, has a distinctly medieval appearance.

HISTORY OF BOLZANO

Mentioned for the first time (as Bauzanum) by Paulus Diaconus in his medieval history of the Lombards, Bolzano formed part of the episcopal principality of Trento in the 11th century and was joined to the Tyrol in the 16th century. The oldest part of the city grew up around the little Romanesque church of San Giovanni in Villa (12th century), but the greatest building activity was that of the Gothic period, when Bolzano became a major mercantile centre. Long a possession of the bishop-princes of Trento, it eventually passed to the Counts of Tyrol, who were succeeded by the Dukes of Carinthia and, after 1363, the Dukes of Austria. The Habsburgs held the city until 1918, except during the Napoleonic period, when it was briefly united first to Bavaria and then to the Napoleonic Kingdom of Italy. In the late 19th century the old city, having remained substantially unchanged over the centuries, grew to include the elegant suburb of Gries. In the 1930s industrial development gave rise to a number of new factories and working-class neighbourhoods towards the west and south, which also changed the city's predominantly German ethnic composition by attracting large numbers of labourers from southern Italy.

THE TOWN CENTRE

The centre of the city is the busy, spacious **Piazza Walther**. It takes its name from a monument erected in the 19th century to the medieval German poet Walther von der Vogelweide, thought to have been a native of the region. The **cathedral**, a Gothic church of the 14th and 15th centuries (restored after 1945), with an elegant apse, a steep tile roof and a fretwork spire, overlooks the square from the south. Fine doorways and reliefs adorn the exterior, and the three-aisled interior has frescoes of the 14th–16th centuries, a fine pulpit with reliefs of 1514, and a great Baroque altar.

The **Chiesa dei Domenicani**, one block west, is the old church of the Italian community in Bolzano. It too was damaged in the war and has subsequently been rebuilt. The interior preserves remains of 14th- and 15th-century frescoes. Over the last north altar is a restored altarpiece by Guercino (1655) and adjoining the apse is the Cappella di San Giovanni, with fine frescoes by followers of Giotto (c. 1340). More frescoes, dating from the 14th–16th centuries, are in the Gothic cloister (*entrance at no. 19a*), the Chapter House and the Cappella di Santa Caterina.

The **Museion-Museum für Moderne Kunst** (*Via Dante 6; open Tues–Sun 10–6, Thur 10–10, with free entry after 6*), with a permanent collection of nearly 5,000 works of modern and contemporary art and an excellent programme of temporary exhibitions, is one of the leading modern art museums in the Alps. The building, a white cube designed by KSV–Krüger, Schuberth, Vandreike (Berlin), has glass front and rear façades and a double pedestrian bridge that link the old town with the park along the River Tàlvera and the new town beyond. The painting and drawing collections are the oldest and most comprehensive of the museum's holdings; they reach back to early 20th-century Expressionism; the other sections focus on more contemporary trends, grouping works under the themes of language in art and New Writing (exploring the relationship between the image and the written word), Zero (the German avant-garde group founded in the 1950s by Heinz Mack and Otto Peine, an important precursor of Conceptual Art), light art, works in space (sculpture and installation art), photography and video. A special section is devoted to the Enea Righi collection, a private legacy focusing on the human body and sociopolitical engagement.

Returning to the church, turn left at the east end of the square to reach **Piazza Erbe**, the site of a colourful fruit and vegetable market. This lively square, at the crossing of two major pedestrian streets, is flanked by fine old houses and adorned, on one side, by the 18th-century Fontana del Nettuno, with a bronze statue by Giorgio Mayr, a local artist. To the east stretches the straight, narrow **Via dei Portici**, the oldest thoroughfare in the city and now also its main shopping street. It is flanked by handsome porticoed houses dating from the 15th–18th centuries, with distinctive bay windows; at no. 39 (the main façade is in Via Argentieri) is the Baroque Palazzo Mercantile (1708), by the Veronese architect Francesco Pedrotti.

From Piazza Erbe, Via dei Francescani winds northwards to the 14th-century Gothic **Chiesa dei Francescani**, with a richly-carved high altar (1500) and a graceful 14th-century cloister with fragmentary frescoes. At the next corner Via Vinfler leads right to the **Museo di Scienze Naturali** (*open Tues–Sun 10–6*), devoted to the landscape and ecosystems of the upper valley of the Adige. Continuing along Via Hofer you take your first left, first right, and first left again to reach **San Giovanni in Villa**, the oldest church in Bolzano, built in the 13th century and enlarged in the early 14th. It has a powerful Romanesque-Gothic campanile and 14th-century frescoes.

Via del Museo, also with elegant shops (and cafés serving unforgettable cakes and pastries) leads west from Piazza Erbe to the **Museo Archeologico dell'Alto-Adige** (*open Tues–Sun 10–6*), displaying antiquities from the Mesolithic to the Roman age. The most outstanding (and disquieting) exhibit is Ötzi, the 5,000-year-old man found mummified beneath the ice of the Similaun Glacier (*map B, A1*), preserved here in a special refrigerated cell. Numerous well-mounted displays show his garments and tools and explain his life and times. Audio tours are available in English.

ÖTZI, THE ICEMAN

Ötzi was discovered in 1991 on the Similaun glacier, at an elevation of 3210m in the Ötztal in Tyrol. The 5,300-year-old traveller was buried soon after his death beneath a thick blanket of snow that was compacted into ice over the centuries, preserving his body, clothing and tools in a near-perfect state. One of the most important archaeological finds of recent years, the Iceman was discovered by chance, on 19th September 1991, by two German hikers who spotted what they believed to be the remains of an unlucky fellow excursionist. Rescue workers who began removal of the body quickly reached a different conclusion: examination of his clothing showed that the man had been dressed in a loincloth, leggings and leather goatskin jacket, his head covered by a cap of bearskin and his body protected by a large mantle composed of alpine grasses. At the time of his death he was carrying some small everyday implements—a scraper, a drill, a bone sewing needle and a small box of embers for starting a fire—as well as a bow, a quiver with some arrows, an axe and a knife. His body bore several tattoos, now believed to be medicinal in nature.

The site of the discovery, the position of the body and the objects that accompany it all suggest Ötzi was not buried, he simply fell when he could go on no further. Various hypotheses have been advanced over the years as to his possible role in the society of his time—hunter, shepherd, warrior, shaman, prospector—as well as the circumstances surrounding the death. In this connection, a particularly important discovery was made in 2001, when X-ray examination revealed an arrowhead lodged in the left shoulder of the corpse. Although the arrow is thought to have travelled a considerable distance before striking its victim, scientists are convinced it still had sufficient impetus to cause an internal haemorrhage and, eventually, death

Carbon dating shows the Iceman lived between 3350 and 3100 BC—

which, some like to say, makes him the oldest mummy in the world. But he is not really a mummy at all. Mummies are embalmed after the removal of their vital organs: the Iceman is the only known example of a human body preserved over the millennia by the power of extreme cold alone. Scientists explain the phenomenon by assuming a spontaneous process of freeze-drying (lyophilisation) due to the specific conditions of the Similaun glacier: low temperature and low humidity.

Immediately after its recovery the body was taken to the University of Innsbruck, partly as a result of uncertainty over the exact location of the site in relation to the Italian-Austrian border, and partly because the laboratories there were perfectly equipped to conduct the necessary analyses. When authority over the archaeological area was acknowledged to the South Tyrol in 1998, the finds were transferred to Italy, where they are beautifully displayed in the archeological museum of Bolzano.

The **Museo Civico** (*open Tues–Sun 10–6*) occupies the former Hullach mansion at the corner of Via Cassa di Risparmio. It contains a regional archaeological collection with finds from the Mesolithic to the Middle Ages, ethnographic material (notably a collection of costumes, household articles and reconstructions of Stuben from old farmhouses), and a picture gallery with works by local artists of the 15th–17th centuries (including numerous shuttered altars and wood sculptures).

GRIES

Ponte Tàlvera crosses the river to the **Monumento della Vittoria**, a huge triumphal arch erected to a design by the Roman architect Marcello Piacentini in 1928. The monument, seen as a provocation by ethnic Germans, has been the object of several terrorist attacks and is now inaccessible. On the river banks are a park with beautiful promenades. That on the east bank leads northwards to join the Passeggiata Sant'Osvaldo, which climbs the slopes of the Renon hill, offering splendid views back over the town and valley. At the foot of the hill the promenade passes the medieval Castel Maréccio, now a convention centre.

West of the Tàlvera, Corso Libertà leads through the Rationalist neighbourhoods of the early 20th-century extension of the city to the garden suburb of Gries. On the main square are the **Benedictine monastery of Muri-Gries**, whose late Baroque church (1771) has frescoes and altarpieces by the Tyrolean painter Martin Knoller, and a little museum displaying antique and modern Christmas cribs. The monks produce excellent wines, which can be tasted on weekdays at the wine bar. A little further on is the old Gothic parish church, with a carved and painted altarpiece by Michael Pacher (1475).

BOLZANO SUD

Bolzano's southern quarters have become one of Italy's most exciting laboratories for experimentation in new architecture. A short walk from the city centre, at Via Roma 20, is the stunning urban campus of the **Scuola Professionale Provinciale per l'Artigianato e l'Industria/Landesberufsschule für Handwerk und**

Industrie, by architects Höller & Klotzner of Merano. The straightforward, no-nonsense design of this new trade school (Alto Adige Architecture Award 2008, Dedalo Minosse Building Award 2008) makes masterful use of structural detail in an unabashed homage to Modernism. Three parallel classroom blocks of different length and height are arranged perpendicular to Via Roma. To the street the blocks present solid concrete or steel-mesh walls broken by only the smallest of windows, but laterally they are faced with continuous glass curtain walls. You can wander into the complex from the square to the north. The centrally located, glass-roofed courtyard is one of the most surprising bits of architecture in Bolzano: here it's easy to see how the pieces fit together; the stairs can be seen behind their thick mesh, and the gym beneath the glass-brick pavement. All accessory facilities—the canteen, library and administration offices—are concentrated in the central block; the classrooms are located in the outer blocks, connected by walkways the windows of which have been decorated with letters and icons by the Austrian artist Heimo Zobernig. A nice touch is the translucent glass louvring that shields the classroom window-walls: the slats can be adjusted to avoid glare inside the rooms. At night and in winter they are closed to form a second skin; in summer they are left open to facilitate overnight cooling.

Huddled like a low stone fortress of spirituality amidst anonymous suburban high-rises, the **Centro Parocchiale Madre Teresa** (Delueg Architekten of Bressanone, 2004–12) at Piazza Firmian 1 makes exemplary use of natural elements—stone, wood, even water—to create an atmosphere of quiet serenity. Within, the minimalist lines are perfectly complemented by the light and colour of Cristoph Hofer's simple but beautiful stained-glass windows. The centre took the Grand Prize and First Prize for Public Architecture at the 2013 Alto Adige Architecture Awards.

Casa Nova is a new, sustainable neighbourhood on Bolzano's southwestern edge (under construction at the time of writing, it is expected to accommodate 3,500 residents in nearly 1,000 dwellings). In order to retain the neighbourhood's green character as far as possible, planners are creating a compact development in the form of eight building courts or *castelli*, a reference to the traditional citadel-like homes of the South Tyolean gentleman farmers. Each *castello* is made up of three or four buildings of varying height and size, with a total of 120 dwellings arranged around a communal garden. An office and retail area is situated in the middle of the neighbourhood. The architecture is understated (especially on the garden side) and the skewed angles of the rooftops (all are slanted southward to increase exposure and minimise shadowing) merge, ideally, with the mountainous panorama. The project design has been entrusted, through international tender, to an interdisciplinary working group coordinated by Dutch architect and planner Frits van Dongen. The reduction of car traffic will be achieved by integrating Casa Nova's pedestrian-bicycle system with that of the city, and constructing a railway station and bus interchange on the line connecting central Bolzano with Merano. Rooftop gardens on every building, a photovoltaic solar energy bank along the railway, centralised steam heating and state-of-the art systems for collection and reuse of rainwater (in the irrigation of parks and gardens, and in flush toilets) will contribute substantially to the neighbourhood's overall environmental quality.

MMM Firmian (*open 1st Sun in March–3rd Sun in Nov daily except Thur 10–6*) at Castel Firmiano, is the temporary exhibition venue of Reinhold Messner's Messner Mountain Museum system (MMM: permanent collections at Brunico, Cibiana di Cadore, Kastelbell, Plan de Corones and Sulden). Also called *Sigmundskron* (after Sigismund, Prince of Tyrol and Archduke of Austria, who resided here in the mid-15th century), the castle is quite large and viewing an exhibition takes you down paths and up stairs, from the depths of the mountains to the castle towers. The design of the museum and castle renovation is by South Tyrolean architect Werner Tscholl (2009), who also oversaw the renovation of the Benedictine abbey of Monte Maria/Marienberg and Castel Fürstenburg near Malles Venosta/Mals. The views over the city and its amphitheatre of vineyards and mountains are magnificent.

AROUND BOLZANO

One of the characteristic features of Bolzano is the amazing number of walks you can take in the immediate environs of the city. The **Passeggiata del Gùncina** winds up the hill behind the parish church in Gries to the Castel Gùncina (476m), with superb views over Bolzano and the Dolomites. The path, cut out of a porphyry wall, is planted with Mediterranean flora. The **Passeggiata Sant'Osvaldo-Santa Maddalena** ascends the hill of Santa Maddalena, with a Romanesque church of Mary Magdalene in a picturesque setting amidst vineyards. It can be followed from Via Sant'Osvaldo to the Lungotàlvera and vice versa. A cableway (*lower station in Via Sarentino*) climbs the 1087m to **San Genesio Altesino**, a busy summer and winter resort on the Altopiano del Salto, with splendid views over the Val Sarentina and the Dolomites. Another cableway starts from Via Renon (near the station) and mounts to Soprabolzano/Oberbozen, on the **Renon/Ritten** highland north of the city. Near Collalbo, the main town of the plateau and an excellent starting point for walks and climbs, are the earth-pillars of **Longomoso**, the most dramatic of the many examples of this curious erosion phenomenon in the area; the path continues to the Rifugio Corno di Renon (2259m, a 3hr ascent), commanding a breathtaking view.

A SHORT DRIVE AWAY

You need a car to reach **Castel Ròncolo/Schloss Runkelstein** (*open Tues–Sun 10–5; map B, B2*), a 13th-century castle on a cliff top at the mouth of the Val Sarentina. Inside are frescoes of late-medieval court life and stories of Tristan and Isolde (in the Palazzo Occidentale, Stua da Bagno and Sala del Torneo), 16th-century scenes of chivalry (in the Casa d'Estate) and a *Martyrdom of St Catherine* (in the 13th-century chapel).

    Terlano/Terlan (*map B, B2*), 10km northwest on the road to Merano, is the centre of a wine-growing district. It has a Gothic parish church with a 15th-century fresco of St Christopher on the façade, and two campanili. **Appiano/Eppan** (*map B, B2*) has several fine 17th–18th-century houses in a local Renaissance style; it lies at the heart of the South Tyrol's famous Strada del Vino, which winds its way among the province's finest vineyards. Above the town rises the castle of Hocheppan, founded in the 12th century, which retains a Romanesque chapel with murals (*open March–Nov Thur–Tues 10–6*). At **Caldaro/Kaltern** (*map B, B3*), on the Lago di Caldaro/ Kalterersee, the Museo Provinciale del Vino (*open April–Nov Mon–Sat 10–5, Sun and holidays 10–12*) occupies the former cellars of the lords of Caldaro-Laimburg. The museum also has its own vineyards, where historical varieties of grapes are grown.

The *chiesa parocchiale* in **Laives/Leifers** (*map B, B3*), 9km south of Bolzano, owes much of its beauty to a 2003 extension designed by Merano architects Höller & Klotzner. A brilliant addition to this small church, in a difficult historical/architectural context, the extension (2004 Alto Adige Architecture Award) is a tent-like wedge that develops along the axis of the existing transept, more than doubling the space of the original building. The extension makes ample use of warm natural maple wood in the interior, is externally faced with weathering copper and connected to the older building by a glazed causeway. Entry to the church is still through the historic building, the nave of which is now the atrium of the new complex.

At **Magré/Margreid** (*map B, B3*) the new volunteer fire station (Bergmeister Wolf Architekten, Bressanone, 2009; *shown weekdays by appointment, T: 0471 817251*) occupies three large caves excavated in the mountainside. A stunning black concrete wall, slightly offset from the sheer rockface but parallel to it in horizontal development and inclination, protects the station and from rock slides. Its surface is broken at rhythmic intervals by three projecting rectangular forms—the glass office block and two black metal doorframes, which seem to launch red fire-trucks into the exterior. The design has drawn a great deal of attention for its approach to land use and energy conservation. The building could have been built outside the mountain, but to do so would have occupied valuable agricultural land; in addition, placement of the facility within the mountain has meant that only the doors are exposed to the outside air (-10°C in winter); the rest of the structure is shielded by the rock (+12° in winter), and large parts of the interior are heated only by the latter's natural warmth. Last but not least, the glazed surfaces of the doors and office cube create a greenhouse effect; the residual energy needed to heat the facility is ecologically produced by a pellet furnace.

THE SCILIAR–CANTINACCIO/SCHLERN–ROSENGARTEN NATURE RESERVE

Park offices: Bolzano, Ufficio Parchi Naturali, Via Renon 4, T: 0471 417770.
Visitor Centre: Tires, Bagni di Lavina Bianca, T: 0471 642196. www.provinz.
bz.it/nature-territory/themes/naturpark-schlern-rosengarten.asp.
The Parco naturale Sciliar-Catinaccio, established in 1974, combines the rocky walls, cliffs and the ledges of the Sciliar Massif with the verdant pastures of the Alpe di Siusi, where traditional human activities are allowed, but new building (including ski-lifts) is strictly limited and the circulation of motor vehicles is forbidden.

The geological history of the Dolomites can be read clearly here. Above the oldest rock, dark-red quartziferous porphyry of the Adige valley are the sandstones of the Val Gardena, which, because of their high iron content, colour the soil of the fields red. Higher up, covered by forests, are rocks that were formed just 65 million years ago, in the Permian and lower Triassic eras. There follow layers of sedimentary and volcanic rock—a clear sign that the coral reefs of the ancient Mediterranean (which over time would become the pink calcium magnesium carbonate, dolomite) were periodically submerged beneath layers of lava and ash (to which highlands like the Alpe di Siusi owe their fertility).

The Sciliar accommodates an extraordinary variety of plant species. In addition to the common alpine flowers (gentians, primroses, crocuses, anemones) you'll find numerous saxifrages (*S. oppositifolia, S. caesia, S. squarrosa*), the so-called *strega dello Sciliar* (*Armeria alpina*), edelweiss, alpine poppies, streaked daphnae, and many, many more. In the forests, keep an eye out for chamois, roe dear, hare and ermine; sparrowhawks and various owls; grouse, white partridge, alpine crows, black woodpeckers, and numerous sparrows.

The park is reached via **Siusi/Seis am Schlern** (*map B, C2*), a summer and winter resort with a pleasant main square, or **Castelrotto/Kastelruth** (*map B, C2*) , a fairytale village huddled around a massive (and loud) 18th-century bell-tower and taking its name from the medieval castle, set on a wooded knoll a short way from the village square. **Tires** and **San Cipriano** are the gateways to the wild Val Ciamin and the adjacent Catinaccio/Rosengarten group, the mythical lair of the dwarf-king Laurin. At **Fiè allo Sciliar** the 13th-century Castel Presule Colonna (*open for guided visits in July and Aug, www.schloss-proesels.it/en/index.php*), rebuilt in 1517, holds a small collection of art and antiques.

THE VAL GARDENA

The Val Gardena is a Ladin-speaking valley reached via **Ponte Gardena/Waidbruck** (*map B, C2*), north of Bolzano on the Brenner road. Wedged between the steep walls of the Val d'Isarco, Ponte Gardena is a rather dark place nestled around the Castel Forte Trostburg, a 12th-century castle of the Wolkenstein, with a 16th-century hall. The Südtiroler Burgeninstitut now maintains a Museo dei Castelli dell'Alto Adige here, with nearly a hundred architectural models of fortified buildings in the province (*open for guided visits Easter–Oct, www.burgeninstitut.com*).

The Val Gardena road winds up and out of the Isarco Valley, through verdant forests and farmland, to **Ortisei/St Ulrich** (1234m; *map B, C2*), a small resort. The 18th-century church here contains good examples of wood-carving, for which Ortisei is noted. The Museo della Val Gardena (*open summer Mon–Fri 10–12 & 2–6, Sun 2–6; winter Wed–Fri 10–12 & 2–6*) has art, craft and natural history collections of local interest.

The road continues to climb, offering a series of changing views over the Sciliar and Puez-Odle peaks. At **Selva di Val Gardena/Wolkenstein** (1563m; *map B, C2*), the Centro Culturale Tublà da Nives is a venue for exhibitions (*opening hours vary* *by event: www.tubladanives.it*). The centre, renovated and enlarged to plans by the young Gardenese architect Rufolf Perathoner (2010), occupies a beautiful, warm old barn and a cool glass annexe. Selva stands at the foot of the Vallunga, which penetrates the heart of the Puez and Gardenaccia mountains to the northeast. The valley ends at the **Passo Sella** (2213m), beyond which lies the Val Badia. The pass has a splendid view, perhaps the finest in all the Dolomites, which takes in the Sasso Lungo (northwest), Sella (northeast) and Marmolada (southeast).

Beyond Ponte Gardena, the Brenner road passes the ancient small town of **Chiusa** (*map B, C2*). The chapel of the Madonna di Loreto contains a precious treasury. On a steep rock nearby rises the **Monastero di Sabiona**, seat of the bishops of Tyrol from the 6th–10th centuries, after which the administrative centre of the diocese was moved to Bressanone. Struck by lightning and destroyed by fire in 1535, it was rebuilt in the 17th century. The monastery, which is still home to a small community of Benedictine nuns, is the destination of a famous—and arduous—triennial pilgrimage by the Ladins of the Val Badia, who cover the 33km and 1800m elevation gain from Longiarù to Sabiona in just one day, returning to Longiarù the following day. The *Prozesciun di Jeunn* takes place in mid-June and outsiders are welcome. A few kilometres northeast of the convent, the fine **Castel Velturno**, built in 1577–87, was the summer residence of the bishop-princes of Bressanone; its beautifully decorated Renaissance rooms hold small but interesting collections of regional paintings and antiquities (*shown on guided tours March–Nov, www.museums-southtyrol. it/en/museums.asp?muspo_id=603*).

THE STRADA DELLE DOLOMITI

The famous Strada delle Dolomiti (Road 241; *map B, C3*) runs from Bolzano on the west side of the Dolomites to Cortina d'Ampezzo on the east. It is one of the most beautiful roads in the Alps, as well as a magnificent feat of engineering. From Bolzano the road enters the wild and romantic gorge of the Val d'Ega, passing the Ponte della Cascata. It then passes the resorts of Nova Levante (1182m) and Carezza al Lago (1609m), dominated by the two most typical Dolomite mountain groups with their characteristic battlemented skyline, the **Látemar** (2842m) and the **Catinaccio** (2981m). The latter is especially famous for its marvellous colouring at sunrise, from which it takes the German name Rosengarten ('Rose Garden'). The road summit is reached at the Passo di Costalunga (1745m), with a splendid view ahead of the Val di Fassa and the Marmolada and San Martino mountains. The **Marmolada** (3342m), the largest and highest group of mountain peaks in the Dolomites, is approached from the Avisio and Contrin valleys by cableways and chair lifts. A winding descent through high pastures brings the road into the Val Cordevole, with the villages of Arabba (1601m) and Pieve di Livinallongo (1475m). A long ascent beneath the ruined castle of Andraz leads to the Passo di Falzarego (2105m), a hotly contested strongpoint in the First World War (ruined fortifications are visible by the roadside), beyond which road descends to Cortina d'Ampezzo.

WHERE TO STAY IN AND AROUND BOLZANO

BARBIANO/BARBIAN (*map B, C2*)
€€ Pensione Briol. Set amidst woods and meadows above Tre Chiese, in the Val d'Isarco, and reachable only on foot or by the owners' shuttle. It is an extraordinary example of New Objectivity (*Neue Sachlichkeit*), the rational, functional style of architecture that developed in the early 20th century in Weimar Germany. Architect and painter Hubert Lanzinger designed the building and its furniture. The size and proportions of the building are determined by the lie of the land, and no material is used that cannot be found locally. Crossing the threshold plunges you straight into the 1920s. Form, space and detail, all are pure and uncorrupted, and nothing is superfluous. Rarely is history so tangible. *Tre Chiese, T: 0471 650125, www.briol.it.*

BOLZANO (*map B, B2*)
€€€ Parkhotel Laurin. Bolzano's oldest and finest hotel is named after the mythical dwarf-king of the Dolomites (whose story is told in the murals of the lovely hotel bar). It is a great chunk of history in a lovely park a stone's throw from the train station and from Piazza Walther. Built in 1909–10 for the grandfather of the current owner, the elegant Jugendstil building still exudes the charm and atmosphere of the Belle Epoque. An essential element of the property is the beautiful garden: 4000m2 of ancient trees, shrubs and flowering plants. A recent renovation by architects Boris Podrecca (Vienna) and Albert Mascotti (Bolzano) has created rooms whose elegant simplicity is equal to the style and demeanour of the building as a whole. The (€€€) restaurant is excellent, as are the (€) salads and sandwiches at the bar. *Via Laurin 4, T: 0471 311000, www.laurin.it.*

CALDARO/KALTERN (*map B, B3*)
€€ Seehotel Ambach. This beautiful modern hotel on the Kalterersee is one of the highest achievements of Othmar Barth (1927–2010), the most influential South Tyrolean architect of the 20th century. Though Barth did not leave a large built legacy, his philosophy concerning the relationship between architecture and landscape (they were one, he argued) had a profound effect on younger architects of the Alpine Arc, a region where nature is forcefully present at every turn. The hotel appears today exactly as it did when it was built, nearly half a century ago. The only difference is, the trees in the lakeside park have grown in the meantime, making the setting even prettier. The structure, whose low, curving form follows the contour lines of the hillside so perfectly as to seem a natural outcropping, is a successful example of Barth's idea of using architecture as a means of landscaping. The Ambach family, who commissioned the building, have worked closely with the architect over the years to preserve the property and protect the particular symbiosis that is achieved between interior and exterior spaces. Great care has been taken to maintain the '70s interior décor, for example, which makes a stay here entertaining as well as relaxing. *Campi al Lago 3, T: 0471 960098, http://www.seehotel-ambach.com.*

RENON/RITTEN (*map B, B2–C2*)
€€€ Parkhotel Holzner. Renon's

finest hotel was built over a century ago, at the same time as the delightful narrow-gauge railway connecting Soprabolzano with Collalbo. The nostalgic Old Austria style of the original establishment has been preserved inside and out, so that the Holzner still has an alluring atmosphere of bygone times. It caters especially to families, with large comfortable rooms, some with original Jugendstil and Thonet furniture, outdoor pool and sauna, tennis courts, a park, play areas for children and a small alpine zoo. A large vegetable garden provides ingredients for the excellent dishes served in the dining room, on the terrace, or at 1908, the hotel's gourmet restaurant. *Soprabolzano 18S, T: 0471 345231, www.parkhotel-holzner.com.*

VILLANDRO/VILLANDERS (*map B, C2*)
€€ **Ansitz zum Steinbock**. This is one of the most important historic buildings in Villandro. At once massive and harmonic, it was probably built in the 13th century as the home of the lords of the land, the Villanderer zu Gravetsch. Its present appearance dates mainly from the 17th century, when it was given its *Erker* (oriels), one in the form of a tower. The magnificent wood-panelled *Stuben* have held a restaurant since 1750 (today the excellent Stainbock Wirtstafern, Restaurant of the Year 2011, *Der Große Restaurant & Hotel Guide*), and on the whole the residence has retained its historic structure over the centuries despite numerous changes of ownership. It was completely (and accurately) restored in the 1980s; since 2002 it has belonged to the Rabensteiner family, who have made it one of the most romantic places to stay in South Tyrol. The view from the panoramic terrace is breathtaking. *Santo Stefano 38, T: 0472 843111, www. zumsteinbock.com.*

WHERE TO EAT IN AND AROUND BOLZANO

ANDRIANO (*map B, B2*)
€€ **Aquila Nera/Swarzer Adler**. This fine old inn has been run by the Mathà family since the late 19th century. Outside, details like the ample roof with wide overhangs and the great porch over the stairs, on two tall round pillars, give the building a rural, agrarian air; within, that atmosphere is maintained by abundant warm wood and good wholesome food. The service is quick and courteous, and care is taken to explain the great local dishes. The rooms are contemporary, full of light and quite comfortable. *Piazza Sant'Urbano 2, T: 0471 510288, www. schwarzeradler-andrian.net.*
BOLZANO (*map B, B2*)

€ **Ca' de Bezzi/Batzenhäusl**. A century or so ago you might have found Sigmund Freud here, lunching with other early 20th-century luminaries: Freud summered at Collalbo, on the Renon highland, and at the turn of the century he frequented the Batzenhäusl's first-floor *Künstlerstübele* together with other artists and intellectuals. The first tavern in this location, at the northern edge of Bolzano's historic city centre, was established 1404 by the Teutonic Order; the place takes its name from the *Batzen*, a coin corresponding to the asking price for a jug of wine. Bombed during World War II then neglected for decades afterwards, the landmarked building was restored in 2002 to make this excellent microbrewery. Batzen Bräu comes in three standard varieties: Batzen Hell (light), Batzen Dunkel (dark) and Batzen Weisse (made from wheat, not barley) and there are seasonal and special beers too. In warm weather you can sit beneath ancient beech trees in the *Biergarten*, and on Wed and Thur evenings listen to jazz in the cellar. *Via Andreas Hofer 30, T: 0471 050950, www.batzen.it.*

€€ **Löwengrube**. As far back as the 16th century, the Löwengrube was a well-known traditional coaching inn in a 13th-century building. The biblical name, conjuring up the prophet Daniel's meal in the lion's den, may also be taken as a veiled reference to the dark-panelled, ground-floor Stube with its stone piers and great green majolica stove. A recent renovation (by award-winning architects Bergmeister Wolf, 2012) has created a new bar and some small, semi-private dining rooms on the first floor. The food is as contemporary as the architecture here, presentation being a major element of every dish. One doesn't go away hungry, though: dessert here is a must. *Zollstange 3, T: 0471 970032, www.loewengrube.it.*

€€ **Vögele**. The old Red Eagle Inn (*Zum Roter Adler*), established in 1277 was frequented by Goethe, among others. The inn is still a favourite of townsfolk, who come for the truly outstanding cuisine, much of it organic (don't miss the *Erdäpfelblattln*, traditional potato fritters), but also to soak up the atmosphere of the place, particularly in the beautiful old *Stuben*, created by master carpenter Josef Lobis, with paintings of Tyrolean folk scenes by the early-20th-century regional artist

Rudolf Stolz. Walk through the door, and you enter the heart of old Bolzano, a place where time seems to stand still. *Via Goethe 3, T: 0471 973938, www. voegele.it.*

CHIUSA/KLAUSEN (*map B, C2*)
€ **Turmwirt**. Gudon is a pretty place in the hills a few kilometres southwest of Chiusa, not far from the Chiusa-Val Gardena exit on *autostrada* A22. The Town Clerk of Gudon built his impressive home in the heart of the village more than three centuries ago, in 1678. Two hundred years later an ancestor of the present owners acquired the property and obtained a license to run it as an inn: the Turmwirt. The atmosphere of the past, beautifully preserved in the fine old *Stuben*, extends also to the delicious regional cuisine, which offers the best in traditional flavours and aromas. Most of the ingredients come from so close by, they could be tossed in through the kitchen window; the *Eisacktaler Weinsuppe* (Val d'Isarco wine soup) is legendary. *Gudon 50, T: 0472 844001,www.turmwirt-gufidaun. com.*

RENON/RITTEN (*map B, B2–C2*)
€€ **Patscheiderhof**. This farm, serving delicious country meals, is famous among *bolzanini* but unknown to outsiders. Most of what is served in the magnificent 17th-century *Stube* is produced within a few hundred metres, including the house wines, Müller Thurgau and Vernatsch. There is summer seating outside with stunning views of the Sciliar and Catinaccio peaks, as well as rooms if you choose to stay overnight. To get here take the Renon cable car up from Bolzano station then the one-car narrow-gauge

railway (Stella/Llichtenstern stop), or walk out from Soprabolzano on the Freud-Weg (30min). *Località Signato 178, T: 0471 365267, www.patscheider-hof.com.*

TERMENO/TRAMIN (*map B, B3*)
€€ **Le Verre Capricieux**. The 'Whimsical Glass' is the new garden bistro of award-winning vintner Elena Walch. The small, free-standing building, a pristine garden pavilion with red porphyry exterior walls, warm wood panelling within and plenty of glass, was designed by the young Gardenese architect David Stuflesser: his client was, herself, an architect before becoming a winemaker. The cuisine is classy and generally light, all the wines are available by the glass and there is a good view over the family's Kastelaz vineyard. *Via Andreas Hofer 1, T: 0471 860172, www.elenawalch.com.*
€€ **Taberna Romani**. This rustic stone-walled tavern was once the cellar of Ansitz Romani, a 16th-century aristocratic residence on Termeno's southern edge that also offers holiday flats. In the heart of the South Tryol's Traminer wine district, host and chef Armin Pernstich serves up gourmet interpretations of traditional South Tyrolean dishes with, of course, fine wines, not the least being the spicy Gewürztraminer from the surrounding hills. Great care has been taken to preserve the original architecture and furnishings, which are key to determining the place's warm historic ambiance. The menu is based on locally-grown organic ingredients, and there is summer seating outside beneath a shady pergola. *Via Andreas Hofer 23, T: 0471 860010, www.ansitzromani.com.*

VILLANDRO/VILLANDERS (*see Ansitz zum Steinbock, p. 37*)

Merano

Merano, in German Meran (*map B, B2*), is famous as a climatic resort and spa, and also a climbing centre and ski resort. Together with Maia Alta and Maia Bassa on the opposite bank of the torrent, it consists mainly of monumental hotels and villas, many of them built at the turn of the last century by Austrian architects, surrounded by luxuriant gardens in a sheltered valley. Spring and autumn are the fashionable seasons for visiting Merano. The inhabitants are mainly German-speaking.

The old main street of the medieval town is the narrow **Via dei Portici**, lined by lovely old houses painted in pastel tones. Beneath its low arcades are excellent shops and the Town Hall (1930). **Merano Arte**, in the Haus der Sparkasse, presents excellent exhibitions of international contemporary art (*open Tues–Sun 10–6*). The interior of this landmarked building, by local architects Höller & Klotzner (2001), features a beautiful light-filled open atrium connecting all four floors, pristine white walls and warm larch-wood flooring. The rooms are used for chamber music concerts as well as exhibitions. Behind Via dei Portici is the well-preserved **Castello Principesco** (*open April–Jan Tues–Sat 11–5, Sun and holidays 11–1*), built by Archduke Sigismund in 1445–80 and containing contemporary furnishings. The arms of Scotland alongside those of Austria recall the marriage of Sigismund with Eleanor, daughter of James I of Scotland. At the end of Via dei Portici is the **duomo**, a Gothic church of the 14th–15th century with a curious battlemented façade, a tall tower (83m) and 14th–16th-century tomb reliefs. Inside are two 15th-century altar pieces by Martin Knoller. Palazzo Mamming, at the top of cathedral square near the parish church of San Nicolò, was at the time of writing being restructured to accommodate the new Museo Civico, which will display archaeological finds, wood sculptures, paintings and crafts of local interest.

Along the River Passirio extend gardens and promenades laid out at the turn of the century. The cheerful **Corso Libertà**, with the most fashionable shops, was laid out before the First World War. It passes the Kursaal (1914), the Neoclassical theatre and several elaborate hotels.

Terme Merano, the immense glass, steel and stone spa complex on the south bank of the river, was designed by the renowned South Tyrolean architect Matteo Thun (2005). The stunning Merano 2000 gondola lift, connecting the city to its Ivigna ski slopes, is the work of the lesser known—but more daring—Bolzano architect Rolando Baldi. The base, intermediate and summit stations, made of glass and concrete with superstructures in ruby-red expanded steel (2013 Alto Adige Architecture Award) are well lighted and especially beautiful on snowy evenings after dark.

AROUND MERANO

To a large extent Merano owes its fame as a spa to the visits in the second half of the 19th century by Empress Elisabeth of Austria, the famous Sissi, who stayed at Trauttmansdorff Castle on a hillside south of the city. A lovely promenade links Merano to the castle, passing eleven points of historical and natural interest along the way. The walk takes about 40mins, plus stops. The award-winning **Trauttmansdorff Botanical Gardens** (Most Beautiful Garden in Italy, 2005; International Garden Tourism Award 2013; *open April–Oct 9–7, 1–15 Nov 9–5, Fri in June, July and Aug 9am–11pm*) make the hike out and back well worth the effort. Here, on a rolling twelve-acre site offering breathtaking vistas of Merano and the surrounding mountains, one may wander through no less than 80 garden landscapes grouped into four distinct groups: forests of the world; Mediterranean 'sun gardens'; wetlands and terraced gardens; and traditional cultivated landscapes of the South Tyrol. Summer concerts are held by the lily pond.

The most popular destination in the environs of Merano is the village of **Tirolo** (*map B, B2*), to the north. Ezra Pound stayed in the Castel Fontana here (reconstructed in 1904), which contains mementos of the poet as well as a local museum of agrarian life (*open April–Nov daily except Tues 9.30–5*). In a superb position on the opposite side of a ravine stands **Castel Tirolo** (*open March–Nov Tues–Sun 10–5; Aug 10–6*), the 12th-century castle of the Counts of Tyrol, which gave its name to the region. With the abdication of Margaret Maultasch, the 'ugly duchess', in 1363, the castle and province passed to the Habsburgs. Damaged by a landslip in 1680, the castle was rebuilt in 1904. A magnificent restoration and extension (1998–2003, Walter Angonese, Markus Scherer and Klaus Hellweger) has created a new home for the Museo Storico Culturale, which shows the history of Tyrol from the Stone Age to the Middle Ages, daily life in the Middle Ages, and contemporary history. The castle hosts two site-specific works of contemporary art: a video installation by filmmaker Carmen Tartarotti offering an original perspective on medieval iconography, and a carved stone pathway by sculptor Gottfried Bechtold. The architectural details of the building itself are remarkable: the Romanesque portals are finely carved, and the two chapels hold marvellous wooden Crucifixes.

The castle of **Scena**, on the hill northeast of Maia Alta, is a 14th-century building restored by the Count of Liechtenstein in 1700. It is privately owned, but there are concerts and theatre performances in the courtyard in summer and the beautifully furnished rooms of the interior are shown on guided tours (*open April–Nov, www. schloss-schenna.com/en/schenna-castle/visiting/*).

THE VAL PASSIRIA AND ANDREAS HOFER

In the pastoral Val Passiria, near San Leonardo (*map B, B1*), is Maso dell'Arena (Sandwirt), the birthplace of Tyrolean patriot and martyr Andreas Hofer (1767–1810). Hofer, an innkeeper and cattle-trader, was one of many Tyroleans who advocated the return of the Tyrol to Austria after it had been ceded to Bavaria in 1805, under pressure from Napoleon. With encouragement from Vienna, Hofer led a band of Tyrolese against Franco-Bavarian troops, and won several victories, only to be sacrificed on the altar of military expediency. After suffering defeat at Wagram, and knowing that Napoleon was advancing on Vienna, the Austrian emperor Franz I was persuaded to sue for peace. The conditions of the treaty were the hand of his daughter in marriage to Bonaparte, and the handing over of Tyrol. Hofer fled to a mountain hideout in his native valley. Betrayed to the French and deserted by his emperor, he was executed at Mantua on the personal order of Napoleon. His house (now a hotel) contains a little private museum.

THE VAL VENOSTA

The Val Venosta is the wide and fertile upper valley of the Adige to the west of Merano, near the Austrian and Swiss borders. It has numerous small summer and winter resorts and fine mountain scenery. Part of the valley lies in the Parco Nazionale dello Stelvio (*see below*).

The summer resort of **Naturno/Naturns** (*map B, B2*) has a little Romanesque church, San Procolo, with remarkable 8th-century mural paintings. From here a minor road winds northwards up the long Val Senales, dominated by the great pyramid of the Similaun (3597m), on the Austrian frontier. Ötzi (*see p. 29*) was found in the glacier on the saddle between the Val Senales and the Venter Tal in Austria.

At **Castelbello/Kastelbell** (*map B, A2*), Castel Juval is the home of mountaineer Reinhold Messner and one of six Messner Mountain Museums in the South Tyrol and the Venetian Dolomites. The museum (*shown on guided tours, 4th Sun in March–30 June and 1 Sept–1st Sun in Nov 10–4*) contains Messner's personal collections of art and artefacts: Tibetan antiquities, paintings of the world's holy mountains, ritual masks, material regarding the epic of King Gesar (of Ling, eastern Tibet), and a Tantra room. There are also a section on Messner's mountaineering expeditions, and a small zoo with mountain animals.

The main place in the Val Venosta is **Silandro/Schlanders** (*map B, A2*), with the valley's highest vineyards (722m). The Val Venosta turns to the north beyond Spondigna/Spondinig, gaining in altitude as it approaches the source of the Adige. The **Castel Coira/Churburg**, above Sluderno/Schluderns (*map B, A2*), is the 13th-century castle of the bishops of Coire. It was restored in the 16th century by the Counts Trapp. **Glorenza/Glurns**, to the west (*map B, A2*), is a typical old Tyrolean town with medieval and 16th-century ramparts and three gates. It is particularly well preserved and draws quite a few visitors. In the **Val Monastero/Münster-Tal**, which extends to the west of Glorenza, is the Calven Gorge: here in 1499 the Swiss defeated the Austrians and won their practical independence of the empire.

PARCO NAZIONALE DELLO STELVIO / NATIONAL PARK STILFSER JOCH

Park offices: Bormio (Sondrio), Via De Simoni 42, T: 034 290 0811. Visitor centres: Trentino–Cògolo di Peio, Via Roma 28, T: 0463 754186; Rabbi, Località Rabbi Fonti, T: 0463 985190; Alto Adige–Prato allo Stelvio, Via Croce

4/c, T: 0473 618212; Martello, Trattla 246, T: 0473 745027; Stelvio, Trafoi 57, T: 0473 612031. www.stelviopark.it.

At Spondigna the Stelvio Pass road diverges to the southwest, leaving the Val Venosta to enter the Parco Nazionale dello Stelvio (*map B, A2*). This immense nature reserve, straddling the boundary between the Trentino, South Tyrol and Lombardy, is the largest national park in Italy (135,000 hectares) and one of the oldest (established 1935). It encompasses the magnificent mountain group of the Ortles-Cavedale, with peaks well over 3000m, and is one of the two designated wilderness areas of northern Italy (the other is the Parco Nazionale del Gran Paradiso in Piedmont). Unlike the other parks of the Trentino and South Tyrol, where an effort is made to safeguard the human as well as the natural landscape, here logging, mining, farming and grazing are discouraged, with a view to allowing the area to return as nearly as possible to a 'natural' (though by no means 'original' or 'virgin') state.

The park authorities maintain a significant number of well-marked trails for environmentally compatible summer sports (hiking, climbing) and winter sports (cross-country and back-country skiing, snow-shoeing). In the last few decades the beauty of the park has been threatened, especially in the area within the South Tyrol, by the construction of new roads, hotels and ski lifts. **Solda/Sulden** (1907m), is one of the most important climbing centres in the upper Adige and a holiday resort. Above rise Monte Cevedale (3769m) and the Ortles (Ortler, 3905m), a magnificent peak, defended by the Austrians throughout the First World War. On the outskirts of the village is **MMM Ortles** (*open 4th Sun in May–2nd Sun in Oct and 2nd Sunday in Dec–1 May daily except Tues 2–6; July–Aug 1–7*), Reinhold Messner's spectacular museum built into the hillside and dedicated to the rugged Ortles landscape and its representation in painting, to the Arctic and Antarctic, to skiing, ice-climbing and polar expeditions, and to the world of ice and its inhabitants. The underground space by Silandro architect Arnold Gapp, in raw concrete lighted by a continuous, crevasse-like skylight, is surprisingly light and airy. A large window offers a stunning view of the Ortler and its glacier. The nearby Yak & Yeti inn, which also acts as the museum visitor centre, offers delicious Himalayan dishes as well as typical local fare. The Flohhaus (Flee Hut) in Sulden, once a refuge for mountaineers, holds a tiny museum annexe with curios from Messner's private collection.

Trafoi (1543m; *map B, A2*) is a summer and winter resort with a magnificent panorama of the Ortles massif. Beyond Trafoi begins the long, winding ascent to the **Passo dello Stelvio/Stilfser Joch** (2758m), generally open only from June–Oct. This is the second highest road-pass in the Alps (12m lower than the Col d'Iseran). This was the meeting-place of the frontiers of Italy, Switzerland and Austria until 1918. There is a good view from the Pizzo Garibaldi (2838m), in German called *Dreisprachenspitze* ('Three Languages Peak') from the meeting of the districts where Italian, Romansch and German are spoken. Sigmund Pohl's 2009 Galleria

> Paramassi, a tunnel open on one side to protect the road from falling rocks, is beautiful as well as practical. A minor road winds over the Giogo di Santa Maria (2502m) to Switzerland.

Malles Venosta/Mals (1051m; *map B, A2*) is an old mountain town with its churches rebuilt in the Gothic style. San Benedetto dates from the 9th century or earlier; it has an important Carolingian fresco cycle. Other medieval remains include the ruined Castel Frölich (near the parish church), the Torre Dross (near the Casa della Cultura), and the Preschgenegg (in Via Winkel), Lichtenegg (in the main square), Goldegg, Pracassan and Malsegg (in Via General Verdross) houses. The large Benedictine abbey of Monte Maria/Marienberg, outside the town, extensively rebuilt in the 17th–19th centuries, preserves frescoes of c. 1160. The former farm wing, now the Abbot Hermann House, has been beautifully restored (to designs by local architect Werner Tscholl, 2007–8) to house a museum, guest rooms and seminar rooms. A Trail of the Hours leads (*in c. 4hrs; moderate*) from the Abbey of Monte Maria to Kloster Sankt Johann in Müstair, Switzerland, a UNESCO World Heritage site with more medieval frescoes. Very close to Monte Maria is Fürstenburg, a ruined 13th-century castle into which Tscholl has fit a gorgeous (and fully removable) agricultural sciences school in glass, steel and wood (2002; *shown weekdays by appointment, T: 0473 836500*). The curvilinear Punibach hydroelectric power station above the village of Planol (Monovolume Architecture & Design, Bolzano, 2011) fits so seamlessly into the hillside that it is almost invisible.

At the north end of the Lago di Resia, below the source of the Adige, stands **Resia/ Reschen** (1525m; *map B, A1*), with a splendid view down the valley of the Ortler group. It was rebuilt when its original site was submerged. The Austrian frontier lies just beyond the Passo di Resia (1507m).

WHERE TO STAY IN MERANO, VAL PASSIRIA AND VAL VENOSTA

GLORENZA/GLURNS (*map B, A2*)
€€ Albero Verde/Grünerbaum. The first mention of this attractive inn on the main square of the smallest city in the Alps dates back to 1732. The quaint old façade is actually the creation of early 20th-century 'restorers', who gave it its crenellations and two large balconies. Inside, a much more recent renovation has been undertaken in a minimalist contemporary style, which fits well with the medieval sobriety of the structure as a whole. No-nonsense minimalism sets the tone in the rooms as well, where natural wood and glass offer a pleasant contrast to pristine white walls and off-white upholstery. *Piazza Città 7, T: 0473 831206, www. gasthofgruenerbaum.it.*

MERANO (*map B, B2*)
€€ Ottmanngut–Suite and Breakfast. The house, at the foot of Monte Benedetto, dates from the 13th century. In 1850 it was bought by the merchant Alois Kirchlechner, whose

heirs opened a pension and restaurant some time before the First World War. The present owners come from the same family and have restored the building in an exemplary manner, creating just the right balance between bourgeois home and charming small hotel. There is a very nice garden, too. *Via Verdi 18, T: 0473 449656, www. ottmanngut.it.*

€€ **Westend**. The Westend first opened 1907, in premises built in the late 19th century near Merano's Passeggiata Lungopassirio. Hotel of choice of the German Expressionist writer Gottfried Benn (1886–1956), who composed a number of his poems here, in 1983 the property was acquired by the Strohmer family, who restored it. The historic establishment now offers spacious and sunny rooms, an elegant Jugendstil dining room and lovely gardens, all steeped in the stylish atmosphere of early 20th-century spa hotels. *Via Speckbacher 9, T: 0473 447654, www.westend.it.*

SAN VALENTINO ALLA MUTA/SANKT VALENTIN AUF DER HAIDE (map B, A1)

€ **Villa Waldkönigin**. The Waldkönigin presents an apparent architectural contradiction: on the one hand, the historic villa, built as a private residence in the early 20th century, and on the other, a modern and functional hospitality wing, with restaurant, most of the rooms and suites, and the wellness area. But the contradiction is only apparent: the landmarked property has been renovated in such a way as to preserve as far as possible the original details of the Jugendstil retreat built for the Jörger family of Merano in 1906. The extension, similar in height and volume, underscores the romantic character of the old building. All in all the solution works well for this dreamy little spa resort overlooking the picturesque Lago di Muta/Haidersee, 1470m above sea level. *Waldweg 17, T: 0473 634559, www.waldkoenigin.com.*

WHERE TO EAT IN MERANO, VAL PASSIRIA AND VAL VENOSTA

LAGUNDO/ALGUND (*map B, B2*)
€€ **Zur Blaue Traube**. This late medieval building with its characteristic glazed loggia is cited as an inn as early as 1454, under the name *An der Viehschaid*. The restaurant is located on the first floor, a convention that was once common, but is now rare. Like the architecture and interior design, the cuisine is a skilful combination of old and new, and offers a mixture of tradition and imagination. A beautiful garden terrace offers outside seating in summer. The desserts are not to be missed. *Strada Vecchia 44, T: 0473*

447103, www.blauentraube.it.

LASA/LAAS (*map B, A2*)
€€ **Alla Corona/Zur Krone**. Lasa/ Laas is a pleasant old village of the Upper Val Venosta known for its marble. This former inn, originally a stop on a 19th-century post route through the valley, is a good example of well-preserved architectural heritage in a delicate historical setting. Tradition and innovation, rural and urban character are nicely balanced: the white-panelled ground-floor *Stube* and its furniture have been painstak-

ingly restored, and the understated elegance of the private dining room downstairs (the *kleine Keller*), created during the renovation, bonds perfectly with the traditional setting. The food is as fine as the atmosphere (the *Grießnockerlsuppe*, and in fact all the dumpling dishes, are exquisite). There is outside seating on the lovely square, and overnight accommodation at a neighbouring *Gasthaus* can be arranged. *Via Nazionale 10, T: 0473 626533, www.krone-laas.it.*

MERANO *(map B, B2)*
€€ **Saxifraga Café–Restaurant–Stub'n**. You'll have to work to reach this place on the hill above old Merano: the quickest way up is by the steps behind the duomo (5–6 mins); the easiest, by the winding Via Galilei or the Gilf or Tappeiner footpaths (20–30mins). But once you get there you'll agree it was worth it. The view spans the rooftops of Merano to the valley and the mountains beyond, and the cuisine is light and refined. The place itself is a *Heimatstil* ('down-home style') chalet of 1909, an idealised, early-Modern interpretation of traditional alpine architecture. Inside, the *Stube* is warm and romantic and the food is exquisite, an ideal combination of tra-

dition and innovation. The same people also run a café by the Kurhaus. Via Monte *San Zeno 33, T: 0473 239249, www.saxifraga.it.*

SAN MARTINO IN PASSIRIA/ST. MARTIN IN PASSEIER *(map B, B1)*
€ **Lamm**. A taproom was opened in 1694 on this former farm, documented since 1390, which has been serving good food and drink ever since. In Napoleonic times local farmers—among them Andreas Hofer—gathered here to play cards and the atmosphere of that era still lingers, thanks to the pride in tradition that has been shared by its many owners. The Restaurant Lamm is now a fine example of the successful combination of outstanding architectural heritage and exquisite cuisine. Everything served in the 200-year-old *Stube* comes fresh from the farm to the table, and most of the meats and cheeses, fruit and vegetables, are organic. If you're looking for local flavour try the homemade *tagliatelle* with mountain herbs and Sexten grey cheese or the grilled organic chicken breast with homemade dumplings and rosemary butter. *Via Villaggio 36, T: 0473 641240, www. gasthaus-lamm.it.*

Bressanone &
the Eastern Alps

B ressanone, in German Brixen (*map B, C2*), stands at the meeting-point of
two Alpine streams, the Isarco and the Rienza, and of two important old
roads, from the Val Pusteria and the eastern Tyrol, and from Brennero
and Austria. Situated in a lovely open landscape of cultivated hills between steep
mountain peaks and green forests and meadows, the city conserves the austere
mark of its history as a centre of a vast ecclesiastical principality. The power of
its bishop-princes in fact lasted 800 years, from the late 10th century to 1803. Its
architecture, monuments and artworks, which embody the full variety of styles
from the Romanesque to the Baroque, carry the singular inflexions of a site on a
cultural frontier.

EXPLORING BRESSANONE

The **cathedral**, built in the 9th century, enlarged in the 13th century, and completely rebuilt in Baroque forms in 1745–90, dominates the shady Piazza del Duomo. The
beautifully preserved interior is adorned with ceiling frescoes by the Austrian artist
Paul Troger, and fine carvings. In the adjacent Romanesque cloister are 14th- and
15th-century frescoes of Old and New Testament scenes and the entrance to the
11th-century baptistery, which hosted the famous council called in 1080 to depose
Pope Gregory VII (Hildebrand) and elect the Antipope Clement III.

The **Palazzo dei Principi Vescovi** is a fortified building, preceded by a moat,
rising in the nearby Piazza del Palazzo. Built in the early 13th century by the
bishop-prince Bruno de Kirchberg, it was several times enlarged and then rebuilt
as a Renaissance château, after 1595, for Cardinal Andrea of Austria. Rendered in
Baroque forms after 1710, it remained the residence of the bishop-princes and the
administrative centre of their feudality until 1803. It has an elegant façade and an
imposing courtyard with 24 life-size terracotta statues representing members of
the Habsburg family. The interior hosts the **Museo Diocesano** (*open Tues–Sun
10–5*), with one of the largest art collections in northeastern Italy. It includes sculptures, paintings and medieval decorative arts from local churches; original furnishings of the bishop's residence and liturgical items from the cathedral; and best of all,
an extraordinary collection of *presepi* (Christmas crêches), ranging in date from the
18th–20th centuries. In the beautiful, peaceful garden, flowers and kitchen vegetables are grown together in surprisingly harmonious beds. There are plans to rede-

sign the area on the other side of the palace as a public park with visitor centre, shop and café-restaurant.

Adjoining Piazza del Duomo on the north, Piazza della Parrocchia takes its name from the 15th century Gothic parish church of **San Michele**, with a spired campanile called the Torre Bianca. Inside are 18th-century frescoes by the Viennese painter Josef Hautzinger. On the north of the church stands the Renaissance **Casa Pfaundler** (1581), a medley of Nordic and Italian elements. From here **Via dei Portici Maggiori**, a lovely old street full of shops, leads westward, flanked by houses of the 16th and 17th centuries, many with crenellated roofs and bay windows. The old town hall, at no. 14, has a painting of the *Judgement of Solomon* in the courtyard. The **Museo della Farmacia** at Via Ponte Aquila 4 (*open Tues–Wed 2–6, Sat 11–4*) has displays documenting 400 years of the history of pharmacy.

At the north of the historic city centre, on the west bank of the Isarco, is the **sport and performing-arts quarter**. Further north, near the hospital, the **Liceo delle Scienze Umane Josef Gasser** and **Scuola Materna** are good examples of the care (and resources) that are being brought to bear on scholastic architecture in the South Tyrol. Designed by Peters & Keller Architekten (Stuttgart) in 2008, the high school and nursery (*shown weekdays by appointment, T: 0472 200883*) are bounded by a residential neighbourhood on one side and by the bright red triple gym designed by Othmar Barth and playing fields by Paul Seeber on the other. The project won a special mention in the Dedalo Minosse International Building Prize.

ABBAZIA DI NOVACELLA/KLOSTER NEUSTIFT
Surrounded by meadows and vineyards 3km north, on the main road to Brennero and the Val Pusteria, is the Abbazia di Novacella/Kloster Neustift (*map B, C2*), a vast complex of monastic buildings ranging in date from the 12th–18th centuries. The church and cloister are open all day, but the library and *pinacoteca* are only shown on guided tours at 11 and 3 (*or by appointment, T: 0472 836189*). Three beautiful marked trails starting near the little Chiesa dell'Angelo Custode in Bressanone make walking to the abbey easy, and you really should make an effort to go this way— as many of the townsfolk do on a warm, sunny Sunday.

The abbey was founded in 1141–2 and now belongs to priests of the Augustinian order. Among the older structures are the circular chapel of San Michele (12th century, fortified in the 16th century); the campanile (12th–13th centuries); the cloister, rebuilt at the end of the 14th century, with frescoes of the same period; the Romanesque chapel of San Vittore, with frescoes of the early 14th century; and the monastery church (Santa Maria Assunta), a Romanesque foundation rebuilt in the colourful Bavarian Baroque form in the 18th century and adorned with exuberant frescoes by Matthäus Gündter of Augsburg, a disciple of Tiepolo. Also noteworthy is the library by Antonio Giuseppe Sartori (1773), with stuccoes by Hans Mussack. It preserves some 75,000 volumes and 14th–15th-century paintings by local artists. The beautiful piazza that greets visitors arriving at Novacella was designed by Markus Scherer (2010). The sleek new Bressanone–Varna ring road, by which the abbey can be reached by car (Modus Architects, Bressanone, 2011), won the 2013 Alto Adige Architecture Award for open-space designs.

THE PUEZ-ODLE / PUEX-GEISLER NATURE RESERVE

Park offices: Bolzano, Ufficio Parchi Naturali, Via Renon 4, T: 0471 417 770.
Visitor Centre: Santa Maddalena di Funes 114a; T: 0472 842523. http://www.
provinz.bz.it/nature-territory/themes/naturpark-puez-geisler.asp.
The Puez-Odle Nature Reserve (*map B, C2*) is situated just south of
Bressanone, in the western Dolomites on the watershed between the upper
Val di Funes and the Val Badia. It includes the towering peaks of the Puez
group and Sasso Putia, as well as the dramatically beautiful Vallunga and
Val di Longiarù. The easiest way to reach the park is from Bressanone, via
the Val di Funes to Santa Maddalena di Funes. Here you'll find a new visitor
centre with a very beautiful and interesting small museum (*open Tues–Sat
9.30–12.30 & 2.30–6; also open Sun in July–Aug*) presenting the reserve's
natural and human history. The elegant white building was designed by
Burger Rudacs Architekten, Munich (2009).

The Puez-Odle mountains are classic Dolomites, dating from the
Mesozoic and Tertiary periods and altered in the Quarternary. On the Côl
dela Soné and Côl de Montijela are more recent strata, dating from the
Jurassic and Cretaceous periods and rich in fossils. As in all the nature
reserves of the South Tyrol, traditional farming and grazing have been
allowed to continue in the low-lying areas and on the high pastures, whereas
the mountain slopes in between are heavily wooded. The most common
trees are stone pine, red fir (especially beautiful on the Putia) and larch
(around Halsl). Vast expanses of mugo pine and rhododendron carpet the
western slopes of the Putia, and heathers, cranberries and blueberries
are not uncommon on the forest floor. In May and June the high pastures
explode with crocuses, snow bells, pasque flowers, primulas and anemones.
These are followed in July by monkshood, hellebore, gentians, bellflowers
and edelweiss. Deer and chamois abound, marmots whistle among the rocks
in the more remote areas, and wood grouse live on the slopes of the Putia.

THE UPPER VAL D'ISARCO

North of Bressanone the upper Val d'Isarco has beautiful scenery and spectacular
views of the mountains. Followed by both the railway and the *autostrada*, the valley
gives access via the Brenner Pass to Austria. For many centuries this has been an
important route over the Alps, and imposing fortifications defend the way. The most
impressive of these is certainly the bleak Austrian **Franzensfeste**, which guards the
point where the Val Pusteria meets the Val d'Isarco, at Fortezza (*map B, C1*). This
is the largest fortification in the Alps, covering some 20 hectares. Built by Franz
von Scholl for Austrian Emperor Francis I in the 1830s, the fort was a munitions
depot until 2003. A costly and beautiful restoration conducted to designs by South
Tyrolean architects Markus Scherer and Walter Dietl (2008–2010) has transformed
it into a cultural centre (*open Tues–Sun 10–6*). A small permanent exhibition focus-
es on the history of the Fortezza and on the concept of a 'fortress' in general, extend-
ing the latter to include such matters as espionage, electronic surveillance and
closed borders.

Vipiteno/Sterzing (*map B, C1*) is a picturesque little town that takes its name from a Roman post established here. It owed its importance to the mines that were worked in the side-valleys until the 18th century. The Palazzo Comunale is an attractive building of 1468–73, and around the tall Torre di Città are 15th–16th-century mansions, many with battlements, built by the old mine-owning families. The Casa dell'Ordine Teutonico, with the **Museo Civico e Museo Multscher** (*open May–Oct Tues–Sat 10–1 & 1.30–5*) contains maps, prints and parts of a beautiful late-Gothic polyptych for the parish church (*chiesa parrochiale*) by the German artist Hans Multscher (1458–59; dismantled in 1779 when the church was remodelled in the Baroque style). The church itself has a presbytery renovated by Siegfried Delueg with sculpted altar and pulpit by Lois Anvidalfarei (2009).

To the northwest of the old town, by the church of Santa Margherita, are Vipiteno's schools. The area is bounded on the south by the long, glass and cedar façades of the new **High School** (Höller & Klotzner, 2002), one of the most attractive in Europe. Across the green is the phenomenal new **Elementary School** by CeZ Calderan Zanovello Architetti of Bolzano, winner of the 2011 South Tyrolean Architecture Award (*both schools shown by appointment, T: 0472 723700*).

Castel Tasso, 3km south of Vipiteno (*map B, C1*), dates from the 12th–16th centuries and has late Gothic decorations (*shown on guided tours April–Oct; T: 339 264 3752*).

North of Vipiteno the valley narrows and its higher slopes are covered with evergreen forests. **Colle Isarco** (1098m; *map B, C1*) is a resort at the foot of the wooded Val di Fléres, once famous for its silver mines. **Brennero** (1375m; *map B, C1*) is the last Italian village, just south of the stone pillar (1921) that marks the Austrian frontier on the Brenner Pass (1375m). This is the lowest of the great Alpine passes, and the flat broad saddle of the Brenner, first mentioned with the crossing of Augustus in 13 BC, was the main route of the medieval invaders of Italy.

THE LOWER VAL PUSTERIA

The Val Pusteria (*map B, C1–D1–D2*), the valley of the Rienza, is one of the most beautiful districts in South Tyrol. In the attractive, brightly coloured villages many of the churches have bulbous steeples and contain good local wood-carvings. The breadth of the valley allows splendid views of the mountains at the head of the side-glens. In the main valley German has replaced Ladin, but in one side-valley (the lovely Val Badia; *see below*) the old language has been preserved. The Val Pusteria has good facilities for cross-country as well as downhill skiing. There are numerous small family-run hotels in the valley, and bed and breakfasts scattered through the countryside.

The entrance to the valley is guarded by handsome castles. **Castello di Rodengo/ Schloss Rodeneck** (868m), a well-preserved 12th-century fortress overlooking the valley of the Rienza near the ski resort of Rio di Pusterìa (*shown on guided tours May–Oct Tues–Sun at 10, 11 and 3; T: 0472 454044*), dates from 1140 (though altered in the 16th century). It contains secular frescoes of c. 1200. **Casteldarne/Ehrenburg** has a 13th-century castle partly rebuilt in Baroque forms in the 18th century. The convent of **Castel Badia/Sonnenburg** (restored as a hotel), with a 12th-century chapel, can be seen on the left on the approach to San Lorenzo di Sebato, a village on the site of the larger Roman Sebatum. The latter has been partly excavated (you can see the walls) and the little **Museo Archeologico Mansio Sebatum** (*open Mon–Fri 9–12 & 3–8, Sat 9–12*) displays finds from the Iron Age to the Roman period. The 13th-century church contains good carvings; a covered bridge still marks the original approach to the village from the Val Pusteria road.

THE VAL BADIA

South of San Lorenzo a winding road with well-designed tunnels leads through a steep, narrow gorge to the Val Badia. This Ladin-speaking valley, one of the most secluded and spectacular of the Dolomites, is widely renowned for its natural beauty and has a number of summer and winter resorts. The most charming of these is **San Vigilio di Marebbe/Al Plan de Maréo** (*map B, D2*), a Brigadoon-like spot at the foot of the Fanes highlands. A smart but quiet place, San Vigilio preserves an air of authenticity despite the vicinity of the Plan de Corones ski slopes, the largest winter sports complex in the region. Zaha Hadid has designed the sixth and final Messner Mountain Museum, to be embedded in the mountaintop at Plan de Corones: the museum is dedicated to the great rockfaces of the world.

On a hillside above San Vigilio is the ancient capital of the Val Badia, **Pieve di Marebbe/La Pli**, still little more than a village, with a parish church and Gothic inn. Here, and throughout the Val Badia, you'll see the lovely old farms known in Ladin as *viles*—small three- or four-family hamlets in wood and stone, some dating back to the 12th or 13th centuries. In the harsh climate and on the difficult terrain of the Dolomites, the life of the inhabitants was based on a unique combination of community organisation and self-sufficiency. Good and bad land was evenly distributed across the farms, creating an ideal balance between seed crops and livestock farming, while woods and high alpine pastures were shared communally. It is the communal approach that distinguishes these ancient settlements from the single farm type, which developed in the late Middle Ages. One is reminded of American Modernist architect Louis Sullivan's famous remark: 'It is the pervading law of all things organic and inorganic, of all things physical and metaphysical, of all things human and all things superhuman, of all true manifestations of the head, of the heart, of the soul, that the life is recognisable in its expression, that form ever follows function. This is the law.' ('The Tall Office Building Artistically Considered', *Lippincott's Magazine*, 1896).

The Museum Ladin Ciastel de Tor housed in the medieval castle of **San Martino in Badia/San Martin de Tor** (*map B, C2–D2*) is perhaps the most fascinating ethnographic museum in Italy (*open Easter–Oct Tues–Sat 10–5, Sun 10–6; July and Aug Tues–Sat 10–6, Sun 2–6; 26 Dec–7 Jan daily 3–7*). Material displays and interactive supports intertwine to paint a complete portrait of the Ladins of the Dolomites and the physical and biological character of the region in which they live. A branch of the museum at **San Cassiano/Sankt Kassian** (*map B, D2*), in the upper Val Badia (*Micurà de Rü Str. 26; open as above; a ticket to one museum gives entry to both*) is dedicated to *Ursus ladinicus*, a new species of cave bear accidentally discovered by a hiker in 1987. A cave amidst the Conturines peaks, at an elevation of nearly 3000m, contained the remains of dozens of individuals of this species, which inhabited the Dolomites 30,000–60,000 years ago. Most of the exhibits deal with the bear and its habitat and displays include a reconstruction of the Conturines cave, complete with a mock sleeping bear.

The upper Val Badia, in Italian Alta Badia, is famous for its World-Cup ski slopes.

THE FANES-SENES-BRAIES / FANNES-SENNES-PRAGS NATURE RESERVE

Park offices: Bolzano, Ufficio Parchi naturali, via Renon 4, T: 0471 417 770. Visitor centre: San Vigilio di Marebbe, Strada Caterina Lanz 96, T: 0474 506 120. http://www.provinz.bz.it/nature-territory/themes/naturpark-fanes-sennes-prags.asp.

Situated between the Val Pusteria on the north and the Val Badia on the west, the park (*map B, D2*) extends eastwards to the Parco delle Dolomiti di Sesto and southward to the Parco Regionale delle Dolomiti d'Ampezzo. Together the three parks form an immense reserve that is unique in the world. The central nucleus of the protected area is formed by the limestone plateaux of Fanes and Senes, separated by the deep furrow of the Val dai Tàmersc and dominated on the north by the Dolomiti di Braies with the Croda Rossa (3148m, the highest peak of the park), the Picco di Vallandro (2839m) and the Croda del Becco (2810m), at the foot of which lies the marvellous Lago di Braies (1493m), a vividly green mountain lake in a remarkable position surrounded by pine woods.

Imposing stratifications of sedimentary dolomite form the geological underpinnings of these mountains. Over these lie deposits of Jurassic limestone (Piccola and Grande Alpe di Fanes, Alpe di Senes, Croda del Becco, Croda Rossa), often marked by dolinas, furrows, etc., caused by water erosion of the porous stone. Here surface waters vanish rapidly in the subsoil, leaving on the plateaux, especially those of Senes and Fosses, a fairly arid environment where streams flow only during summer storms and spring thaw.

This fact determines a marked contrast between the high central areas, with scarce plant cover, and the lower regions, on the mountainsides and in the valleys, where the waters re-emerge: these are covered by dense forests of red fir, alternating, at the higher altitudes, with larch and cembra pine. Further up, beyond the low growths of scrub pine, rhododendron and whortleberry, the alpine meadows, rocks and rubble are populated by a rich alpine flora that includes the endemic Alpine poppy (*Papaver rhaeticum*), Alpine toadflax (*Linaria alpina*), bear's ear (*Primula auricula*), horned rampion (*Physoplexis comosa*) and the variety of houseleek *Sempervivum dolomiticum*, as well as saxifrages, androsace (rock jasmine), edelweiss and many other species.

The park's fauna includes roe deer, chamois and small colonies of ibex in the area of the Croda del Becco. There are also the classic alpine mammals (marmots, hare, ermine, weasel), amphibians (the alpine frog, *Rana temporari* and alpine newt, *Triturus alpestris*) and a wide variety of birds: royal eagles, kestrel, owls, crows, grouse, white partridge, red woodpeckers, wall creepers (*Tichodroma muraria*), crossbills, alpine finches (*Carduelis citrinella*), water pipits (*Anthus spinoletta*), firecrests (*Regulus ignicapillus*) and crested tits (*Parus cristatus*).

BRUNICO AND THE ALPI AURINE

Brunico/Bruneck (*map B, D1*) is the picturesque capital of the Val Pusteria. It stands in a small upland plain with fir trees and is overlooked by the castle of Bruno, the 13th-century bishop of Bressanone who is traditionally credited with founding it. Brunico is the native town of Michael Pacher (c. 1430–98), whose sculpted wooden crucifixes can be found in the churches of the region. The main Via di Città is lined with pretty alpine houses with bay windows and fanciful gables; many of the shops have old (or old-fashioned) wrought-iron signs.

The castle, on a hill, was built in the 13th and 14th centuries and altered in the 15th and 16th. It now hosts the fifth of Reinhold Messner's six mountain museums, **MMM Ripa** (*open 15 May–1 Nov 10–6 and 26 Dec–25 April 12–6*). The splendid exhibits focus on the mountain peoples of Asia, Africa, South America and Europe, their cultures and religious traditions. The museum design (EM2 Architekten, Brunico, 2011) won the 2013 Alto Adige Architecture Award for Renovation.

In the suburb of Teodone/Dietenheim, on the Mair am Hof farm, is the **Museo Provinciale degli Usi e Costumi** (*open Easter–Oct Tues–Sat 10–5, Sun and holidays 2–6; also open Mon 10–6 in Aug*), an open-air museum of local agricultural methods and folk customs featuring the Baroque Mair am Hof residence, several farmhouses and barns, and exhibits of regional material culture.

North of Brunico, the Val di Tures provides access to a group of thickly wooded mountain glens lying beneath the peaks and glaciers of the Alpi Aurine on the Austrian frontier. **Campo Tures/Sand in Taufers** (*map B, D1*) is the main centre in these valleys, visited by climbers and skiers. It is dominated by the 13th–15th-century castle of the barons of Tures (*shown on guided tours; T: 0471 982255*). The road from Brunico passes a new public spa where outdoor and indoor spaces have been brilliantly orchestrated by architect Christoph Mayr Fingerle; it takes its name, Cascade, from the beautiful Cascate di Riva, above the town. An moderately challenging trail offers spectacular views of the three consecutive falls, which range from 10 to 40m in height. In the Valle Aurina is the peak of the **Vetta d'Italia** (2912m), the northernmost point in Italy. The **Picco dei Tre Signori** (3498m), further east, marked the junction of the counties of Tyrol, Salzburg and Gorizia.

THE VEDRETTE DI RIES–AURINA/RIESERFERNER–AHRN NATURE RESERVE

Park offices: Bolzano, Ufficio Parchi Naturali, Via Renon 4, T: 0471 417770.
Visitor Centre: Nuovo Municipio del Comune di Campo Tures, T: 0474 677546.
http://www.provinz.bz.it/nature-territory/themes/naturpark-rieserferner-ahrn.asp.
Established in 1989, the Vedrette di Ries–Aurina Nature Reserve (*map B, D1*)

extends between the Val Pusteria and the Valle di Anterselva on the south, the Val di Tures on the west, the Valle Aurina on the north and the Austrian border on the east. In addition to the crystalline Riesenferner group, the park includes the southwest slopes of the Durreck Massif. These mountains constitute a small subgroup of the chain of the Alti Tauri (Hohe Tauern), with a dozen peaks over 3000m and some fine glaciers on the northern slopes.

The rocks that form much of the Riesenferner group are Palaeozoic gneiss and schist. Glaciers have deeply moulded these mountains, transforming the heads of the valleys into glacial cirques, carving grooves in the mountain walls, accumulating moraines along their path and hollowing in the rock the niches now occupied by numerous high mountain lakes. Lower down, the streams have formed spectacular gorges and cascades like the Cascate di Riva, near Campo Tures. Among the geological peculiarities of the park are the erosion pyramids (*Platten*) on the right orographic side of the Val Pusteria. At the head of the Valle di Anterselva is the Lago di Anterselva, formed by the alluvial cones that descend the southern slope of the Collalto and the Rotwand. At the entrance to the same valley, but outside the borders of the park, is the Rasun wetland, frequented by migratory birds.

A continental climate and the siliceous nature of the soil are the main influences that have shaped plant life in the Riesenferner group. The most common tree in the forests is the red fir, in the shadow of which rhododendron and whortleberry form a sort of underwood. Larches grow on the sunnier slopes. The most beautiful flowers in the park—which include arnica, bellflowers, anemones, dwarf primrose, edelweiss, dwarf gentian, saxifrages and artemisia—grow in the high-mountain meadows and amid the rocks and rubble at the foot of the peaks.

The forests are populated by roe deer, badgers, fox, marten, squirrels and several native species of birds (notably crossbills and spotted nutcrackers). It is also possible to spot royal eagles, grouse, owls, marmots, chamois, white partridge, ermine and the alpine finch. The invertebrate population includes some beautiful butterflies.

THE UPPER VAL PUSTERIA

The Val Pusteria opens out at Rasun and the three interlocking villages of **Valdaora** (Valdaora di Sotto, di Mezzo and di Sopra; *map B, D1–D2*), each with a church. If you come by train you'll get off at the warm, wooden Bahnhof building serving Valdaora and the Valle d'Anterselva; designed by Walter Dietl of Silandro, it won an architectural award in 2011. In the lovely **Val Casies** are the picturesque 12th-century castle of Monguelfo, with a tall tower, and **Tesido**, a pretty village on the lower sunny slopes of the hillside with two delightful churches, one Baroque, with a pink exterior, and the other—older—with a large external fresco of St Christopher.

Dobbiaco/Toblach (1256m; *map B, D2*) has a large church and a castle built in 1500 for the emperor Maximilian I. Gustav Mahler spent the summers of 1908–10 here, composing his Ninth and Tenth symphonies and the beautiful *Das Lied von der Erde*, in a little cabin in the woods.

San Candido/Innichen (1175m; *map B, D2*) is a lovely little summer and winter resort, with a Baroque parish church. The 13th-century Collegiata (tower 1326), the most important Romanesque church in the South Tyrol, with beautiful sculptural details, is dedicated to Sts Candidus and Corbinian, who are depicted in the fresco by Michael Pacher above the south door. The 15th-century atrium protects the main portal with Romanesque carvings. In the interior is a splendid *Crucifixion* group above the high altar (c. 1200). The remarkable frescoes in the cupola date from c. 1280. The crypt has handsome columns, and there is a small museum open in summer. San Candido's pedestrian zone, with its unique lighting effects (best after dark), won an award for the Viennese architectural firm AllesWirdGut (2002–7), who also designed the striking Ziv (Zivilschutzzentrum, accommodating the volunteer fire brigade, emergency medical service and mountain rescue service) on the town's eastern edge.

East of San Candido the Dolimiti di Sesto take their name from the village of **Sesto/Sexten** (*map B, D2*), a small summer and winter resort with a Baroque parish church (San Vito), frescoed houses, and a small museum with works by local painter Rudolf Stolz (1874–1960).

THE TRE CIME/DREI ZINNEN NATURE RESERVE

Park offices: Bolzano, Ufficio Parchi Naturali, Via Renon 4, T: 0471 417 770.
Visitor Centre: Dobbiaco, Centro Culturale Grand Hotel Toblach, Via Dolomiti 1, T: 0474 973017. http://www.provinz.bz.it/nature-territory/themes/naturpark-sextner-dolomiten.asp.

Seen from the Val Pusteria, the landscape of this park is indescribably dramatic. In the foreground are the subgroups of the Baranci and the Tre Scarperi, among which open two parallel valleys (Val di Dentro and Val Fiscalina) closed at their upper ends by the spectacular vertical walls of the Tre Cime di Lavaredo (2999m), Paterno (2744m), and Cima Dodici (3094m).

The oldest rocks of this last northeastern bastion of the Dolomites are conglomerates of porphyry and sandstone, buried beneath layers of black limestone, dolomite and grey marl. During the Ice Age the region was almost completely buried beneath a gigantic glacier, which has left clear signs of its presence—particularly in the Valle del Rio Alto Fiscalina, where you can see moraines and streaked and round-backed rocks formed by the retreating ice.

The forests here are composed mainly of red fir mixed with larch and a few rare white firs and cembra pines. Sylvan pine grows in groups in the Val di Landro on the more arid slopes. Above the tree line, scrub pine and rhododendron abound. Interesting semi-natural environments are the prati a larice (larch meadows) of the Val Fiscalina and Val Campo di Dentro. The flora includes several species of gentians (for example, *G. punctata* and *G. asclepiadea*), saxifrages (*S. squarrosa, S. oppositifolia, S. caesia*), edelweiss and alpine poppies, just to mention a few. Fauna includes the alpine bat (*Hypsugo savii*), which is found in the forests and even above the tree line.

| Among the numerous species of birds are royal eagles, sparrow hawks, goshawks, falcons, owls, grouse, white partridge, the black woodpecker, and some 70 songbirds.

WHERE TO STAY IN BRESSANONE AND THE EASTERN ALPS

BRAIES (*map B, D2*)
€ **Hohe Gaisl**. This fabulous old lodge is stunningly set at 2000m, directly in front of the Croda Rossa peak (*Hohe Gaisl* in German). It is in the middle of the Fanes–Senes–Braies Nature Reserve, so cars are outlawed (except at arrival and departure). Instead, cross-country skis and sledges are provided in winter, and there is an endless variety of summer walks. The hearty can even hike into Cortina and back (full day required, elevation gain/loss 800m). You won't find much in the way of nightlife here, but after a vigorous day in the crisp mountain air that may not be an issue. The food is exquisite; the sky on clear winter nights, unforgettable. *Località Prato Piazza, T: 0474 748606, www.hohegaisl.com.*

BRESSANONE/BRIXEN (*map B, C2*)
€€ **Aquila d'Oro/Goldener Adler**. Beautiful rooms and warm, cosy public spaces are the hallmarks of this excellent small hotel in an expertly restored historic building in the town centre. Run by the same people who own the Oste Scuro restaurant, Hermann and Maria Mayr, it equals the latter in taste and refinement. The Goldener Adler has been an inn for a very long time: it is mentioned for the first time in documents dating from the 14th century. The 19th-century crenellated exterior has been preserved in full;

within, a measured mixture of ancient and modern creates a pleasantly relaxing atmosphere. There is a spa on the top floor and the ground-floor public spaces are used for exhibitions, talks and other cultural events. *Adlerbrückengasse 9, T: 0472 200621, www.goldener-adler.com.*

€€€ **Elephant**. In a 16th-century building with a large garden and the city's most renowned restaurant, the Elephant is a fine in-town hotel with the charm of a country residence. It takes its name from an pachyderm that stopped here en route from Africa to Vienna, in 1551. The Heiss family has run the hotel for a century and a half, gradually transforming it from a simple inn to a luxury establishment catering to a sophisticated clientèle. There is a clever combination of old and new, showing the greatest respect the ancient architecture, and antiques, paintings and other precious art objects are scattered everywhere. *Via Rio Bianco 4, T: 0472 832750, www. hotelelephant.com.*

€€ **Pupp**. The bold contemporary lines of this hotel at the northern edge of the historic city centre deliberately recall a cairn marking the boundary between the old town and the new. Local architects Christian Scweinbacher and Bergmeisterwolf (2011) have stacked the storeys like stones, with public spaces on the ground floor and rooms and suites, some with private terraces, on the floors above. All rooms are spacious and elegantly furnished, and the hotel's overall atmosphere is bright and cheerful. The famed Pupp café and pastry shop across the street is universally acknowledged by the residents of Bressanone to be the town's finest. Enjoy the sleek minimalist lines, rich textures and bright colours of the building and its furnishings after ten, if you will: the early morning must be reserved for the breakfast buffet. *Altenmarktgasse 36, T: 0472 268 355, www.small-luxury.it.*

SAN LORENZO/ SANKT LORENZEN (map B, D1)

€€€ Schloss Sonnenburg. This was the home of the Abbess Verena, lady of Marebbe and arch-rival of the Renaissance humanist bishop-prince of Bressanone, Cardinal Nicolaus Cusanus (their story is told in a delightful battle of talking portraits in the Ladin Museum at San Martino). From the 11th century onward, Sonnenburg was a Benedictine nunnery where the best noble families of Tyrol sent their unmarried daughters. The convent was repeatedly enlarged and remodelled over the centuries, so that the oldest surviving buildings today are the late-medieval church, with Romanesque paintings in its crypt, and the fortified core of the old cloister. Long simply a country manor, in the 1960s the abbey was purchased by the present owners and made into an upscale hotel and spa. The rooms are large and very well appointed, and together with the beautifully finished public spaces may bring you to revise your idea of the hardships of monastic life. The restaurant is everything one would expect in such circumstances, and the lovely grounds hold a special surprise: the abbess's medicinal herb garden, restored. *Castelbadia 38, T: 0474 479999, www. sonnenburg.com.*

SAN VIGILIO DI MAREBBE/AL PLAN DE MARÉO (map B, D2)

€€ Monte Sella. A delightful Jugendstil villa built at the turn of the century and tastefully renovated, the Monte Sella offers historic ambiance in one of the most beautiful villages in the Dolomites. The proprietors, Norbert and Anna Cristina Cristofolini, are warm, experienced hoteliers, thoroughly acquainted with their territory; the chef is one of the best in the Dolomites and there is a beautiful spa with a strong emphasis on natural cures. Jugendstil rules the rooms of the main building; rooms in the new wing are quietly contemporary. *Strada Catarina Lanz 7, T: 0474 501 034, www. monte-sella.com.*

SAN CANDIDO/INNICHEN (map B, D2)

€€ Orso Grigio/Grauer Bär. Set in the historic centre of San Candido, the Orso Grigio is one of the South Tyrol's oldest inns: its origins date back to the mid-14th century, and it has been in the same family for 250 years. Here you'll find great, thick walls, Gothic vaulted ceilings and rich wood panelling skilfully blended with the new to create an atmosphere of refined comfort. The restoration of 2002–7, a joint venture of architect Christoph Mayr Fingerle and artist Manfred A. Mayr, optimises functional organisation while conveying a feeling of continuity. Mayr's use of colour is particularly well orchestrated. Expect time-honoured aromas and flavours in the excellent gourmet restaurant, too. *Via Rainer 2, T: 0474 913115, www.orsohotel.it.*

SESTO/SEXTEN (*map B, D2*)
€€ **Tre Cime/Drei Zinnen**. Designed in 1930 by Viennese architect Clemens Holzmeister assisted by South Tyrolean artist Rudolf Stolz, this is a major work of Tyrolean Modernism and a pioneering achievement of alpine tourism. The architecture weds traditional vernacular elements with *Neue Sachlichkeit*, the style of art and architecture that developed in Germany in the 1920s and early 1930s. The recent restoration, a collaborative project of architect Christoph Mayr Fingerle and visual artist Manfred A. Mayr (who also worked together at the Orso Grigio in San Candido), took more than a decade to complete (1992–2007) but has preserved the hotel's historic character. The hotel has belonged since it was built to the Watschinger family. *Via San Giuseppe 28, T: 0474 710321, www. hotel-drei-zinnen.com.*

€€ **Chalet Alte Post**. A brilliant example of historic alpine-style hotel architecture magnificently sited amidst larch groves and flowering meadows in the Val Fiscalina, at the foot of the famous Tre Cime/Drei Zinnen. Built in 1906–7 as the Post-Gasthof Fischleintal, it used to be the terminus of the coach route from San Candido. It became an annexe of the larger Hotel Dolomitenhof, next door, when the latter was built in the 1950s.

A fine example of *Heimatstil*, the 20th-century movement in architecture, interior decoration and the decorative arts aimed at protecting and promoting autochthonous regional character, this has been a landmarked building since 1986 and retains its authenticity. The rooms, all with wood floors and many with balconies, are warm and comfortable; amenities (spring-fed pool, restaurant, spa) are shared with the Dolomitenhof. *Via Val Fiscalina 33, T: 0474 713000, www.dolomitenhof.com.*

VIPITENO/STERZING (*map B, C1*)
€€ **Aquila Nera/Schwarzer Adler**. The main building of this large hotel in the heart of Vipiteno dates from the early 15th century; the twin-winged addition in front of the old Town Hall came a hundred years later, and the modern annexe, with indoor pool, sauna and solarium, was added in the late 20th century. For four generations warmth, elegance and comfort have been the key ingredients of the Mühlsteiger family's hospitality; the ground-floor café and the first-floor Stuben offer cosy respite from the cold of winter and the rooms and suites (split between the main building and the annexe) are tastefully decorated and extremely comfortable. Vipiteno's traditional Christmas Market (now less authentic than it once was) is held in the square in front of the hotel in Nov–Dec. *Piazza Città 1, T: 0472 764064, www.schwarzeradler.it.*

WHERE TO EAT IN BRESSANONE
AND THE EASTERN ALPS

NB: Many of the hotels in the above section also have restaurants.

BRESSANONE (*map B, C2*)

€€ **Oste scuro/Finsterwirt**. As far back as 1743, this establishment served the wine delivered as a tithe to the chapter of the cathedral, just a few steps away. The tavern was strictly regulated and had to stop serving at dusk: hence the eloquent name 'The Dark Hostelry', referring to the prohibition of lighting lamps to extend the revelry after dark. Now an extremely fine Tyrolean restaurant, the Oste Scuro/Finsterwirt is known as much for its historic *Stuben* as for its delicious regional dishes, accompanied by fine wines. Wood panelling, antique furniture and original paintings and stained-glass windows create an environment of rare beauty. There is also a lovely garden for the warm months. Rooms down the way at the Aquila d'Oro, under the same management. *Vicolo del Duomo 3, T: 0472 835343, www.finsterwirt.com.*

SAN CASSIANO (*map B, D2*)

€€€ **La Siriola**. La Siriola, the Nightingale, is famous for its delicious, creative interpretations of traditional Ladin cuisine. Local ingredients figure prominently, and guests even get a Ladin glossary. All dishes can be matched with fine wines by the glass and, *dulcis in fundo*, there is a Chocolate Room offering after-dinner tastings of dozens of varieties of chocolate. *Hotel Ciasa Salares, Strada Prè de Vì 31, Località Armentarola, T: 0471 849445, www.siriolagroup.it.*

SAN LORENZO/ST. LORENZEN (*map B, D1*)

€€ **Saaler Wirt**. The origins of Saaler Wirt date back to the late 1500s. It was built as an inn for pilgrims and carters in a beautiful and strategic position on what was once the main road linking the Val Pusteria with Marebbe and the Val Badia, a stone's throw from the little church of Maria Sares. The splendid *Stuben* date from the 1730s and are the house's main architectural asset—but certainly not the only reason to stop in this friendly country hotel/restaurant, now in an idyllic spot far from the main road, which moved to the valley floor long ago. The meat and vegetables, herbs and dairy products come from the family farm and everything, including the baked goods, is home-made. There is summer seating on a covered terrace. *Sares 4, 0474 403147, www.saalerwirt.it.*

SAN VIGILIO DI MAREBBE/AL PLAN DE MARÉO (*map B, D2*)

€ **Ostaria Plazores**. This family restaurant in a 16th-century *Ansitz* offers exquisite cuisine from the Ladin tradition and a good selection of wines. The meat dishes are superb, using beef and lamb raised on the family farm. There is a cosy wood-panelled *Stube* for winter (or cold, cloudy summer days), but in fair weather the kitchen moves to the former bread oven, outside, and meals are served in the garden. *Via Plazores 14, T: 0474 506168, www.plazores.com.*

Practical Information

ARRIVAL AND GETTING AROUND

By air: If you're flying to the Trentino-Alto Adige/South Tyrol, any northern Italian airport east of Milan will do. The most popular choices are Verona, Treviso and Venice. Munich and Innsbruck are also good, as there are excellent rail/bus connections to both. Bolzano has a small regional airport, but it's only served by a flight or two a day, from Rome.

By rail: Bressanone, Bolzano, Trento and Rovereto are major hubs on the north–south artery between Munich and Rome. They're served by high-speed Eurostar and Intercity trains, and regional trains and superb new extra-urban buses radiate outward from their stations to more remote locations (*for Italian railways, info and timetables, see www.trenitalia.com. For integrated rail/bus transport, see www.sii. bz.it/en and www.ttesercizio.it/Extraurbano*).

By car: Any navigation app will tell you how to reach your destination, but you might want to know about traffic en route. You'll find an easy-to-read, real-time map of traffic flow on *www.tuttocitta.it/traffico/trentino-alto-adige* and webcams on *www.meteoindiretta.it/webcam_sezioni.php?id_sezione=9&rid=13*. The latter will also give you the weather.

DRIVING IN ITALY
Regardless of whether you are driving your own car or a hired vehicle, Italian law requires you to carry a valid driving licence. You must also keep a red triangle in the car (you can hire one from ACI for a minimal charge and returned it at the border).

As 80 percent of goods transported travel by road, lorries pose a constant hazard on, and the degree of congestion in even the smallest towns defies imagination.

Certain customs differ radically from those of Britain or America. Pedestrians have the right of way at zebra crossings, although you're taking your life in your hands if you step into the street without looking. Unless otherwise indicated, cars entering a road from the right are given precedence. Trams and trains always have right of way. If an oncoming driver flashes his headlights, it means he is proceeding and not giving you precedence. In towns, Italian drivers frequently change lanes without warning. They also tend to ignore pedestrian crossings.

ROADS IN ITALY

Italy's motorways (*autostrade*) are indicated by green signs or, near the entrance ramps, by large boards of overhead lights. All are toll-roads. At the entrance to motorways, the two directions are indicated by the name of the most important town (and not by the nearest town), which can be momentarily confusing. Dual-carriageways are called *superstrade* (also indicated by green signs). Italy has an excellent network of secondary highways (*strade statali, regionali* or *provinciali,* indicated by blue signs marked SS, SR or SP; on maps simply by a number).

PARKING

Many cities have closed their centres to traffic (except for residents). Access is allowed to hotels and for the disabled. It is always advisable to leave your car in a guarded car park, though with a bit of effort it is almost always possible to find a place to park free of charge, away from the town centre. However, to do so overnight is not advisable. Always lock your car when parked, and never leave anything of value inside it. Many car parks operate the '*disco orario*' system, which allows you to park free for 2hrs. You indicate the time that you parked on the adjustable disc. Hire cars are usually fitted with a disc in their windscreens. They are also available at petrol stations and tobacconists. Many hotels allow special access for customers' cars to restricted central streets.

TAXIS

These are hired from ranks or by telephone; there are no cruising cabs. Before engaging a taxi, it is advisable to make sure it has a meter in working order. Fares vary from city to city but are generally cheaper than London taxis, though considerably more expensive than New York taxis. No tip is expected. Supplements are charged for late-night journeys and for luggage. There is a heavy surcharge when the destination is outside the town limits (ask roughly how much the fare is likely to be).

LOCAL INFORMATION

The autonomous provinces of Trento and Bolzano spend a lot of money on marketing, so there is an excellent, capillary tourist information system in each. From the province websites you can link to the websites of the various tourist consortiua (Val Gardena, Alta Badia, etc.), or connect directly to the tourist office in the town you're planning to visit. Start here:

Trentino (*http://www.visittrentino.it/en*); Alto Adige (South Tyrol; *www.suedtirol. info/en*).

For information on the Dolomites World Heritage site, go to *http://whc.unesco. org/en/list/1237* or *www.dolomitiunesco.info/en/*.

Trento-Rovereto Card

The Trento-Rovereto Towns of Culture Card gives free entry to museums in Trento and Rovereto, and unlimited use of urban and extra-urban buses, trains and cable cars. It provides discounts at performing-arts events and festivals, and free tastings of Trentodoc Metodo Classico sparkling wine and discounts on a variety of local products in participating wine bars, restaurants and shops. Cards are valid for 48 hours, but you can extend the validity to three months or transform it into a 'family card' on request, without paying an additional fee. The card can be purchased at tourist information offices and museum ticket counters, and it is activated on first use: you simply show it when entering a museum, hold it in front of the electronic ticket reader on local public transport, validate it in the electronic ticket readers at railway stations, or show it before ordering/making a purchase at wine bars, restaurants and shops. Expired tickets can be recharged for use on public transport by taking it to a Trentino Trasporti ticket office and loading it for the amount you choose. The card will become a prepaid deduction card for use on urban and extra-urban transport. For full terms and conditions (and an online purchase option), see *www. trentorovereto.it/info.aspx*.

Museumobil Card Südtirol/Alto Adige

The Museumobil Card combines free travel on the Alto Adige's Integrated Public Transport network with free admission to museums in the province. It comes in three-day or seven-day versions, each one for adults and children 0–6, or juniors (7–14). The transport network includes regional trains (not Eurostar/Intercity) on the Brennero–Trento and Malles/Mals–San Candido/Innichen lines; all urban and extra-urban bus services; the Renon/Ritten, Maranza/Meransen, San Genesio/Jenesien, Meltina/Mölten and Verano/Vöran cable cars; the Renon/Ritten narrow-gauge railway and the Mendola/Mendel cable railway and the PostBus Switzerland between Malles/Mals and Müstair. Nearly a hundred museums throughout the province offer one free admission to cardholders; extra services such as guided tours, educational activities or special events are not included unless expressly indicated. The card is non-transferable and must be validated at the beginning of each journey—before boarding when travelling with trains or ropeways—or at each museum entry. The expiry date will be printed on the card at the first validation. Cards may be purchased at any Alto Adige Integrated Transport ticket office (including automatic ticket machines in most railway stations), as well as at tourist offices and many hotels. Full details on *www.mobilcard.info/en/museumobil-card.asp*.

Other visitors' cards

South Tyrol also offers a simple Mobilcard (*www.mobilcard.info/en/mobilcard.asp*) with public transport but without museums and a Bikemobile Card (*www.mobilcard.info/en/bikemobil-card.asp*) coupling public transport and bike rental.

In addition, local visitors' cards are available in many locations. The Brixen Card (*www.brixencard.info/en*) is included in the price of your hotel if you stay in Bressanone (ask for it at the desk) and offers many of the same advantages as the Musemobil Card, plus free admission to the town's Acquarena spa, guided tours in Bressanone and its environs, and guided hikes in the mountains. The MeranCard and Merano Guest Card (*www.meranerland.com/en/holiday-information/advan-*

tage-cards) offer similar benefits. The Val Gardena Card (*www.valgardena.it/en/ hiking-biking/val-gardena-card*) gives six days' unlimited free use of all lifts in Val Gardena open in summer. The price is steep but includes a Mobilcard. It is available at hotels and Val Gardena tourist offices. My Dolomiti Skicard (*www.dolomitisuperski.com/en/ski-pass/purchase-ski-pass/my_dolomiti-skicard*) is a personal chip card issued by the Dolomiti Superski consortium (500km of slopes) that can be recharged with ski passes as many times as desired—in the ski-pass office or online—keeping you out of the queues and on the slopes. The system transfers the booked skiing days at first contact with the reading device at the lift facility onto your personal, non-transferable card and gives automatic access to all lift facilities. The card is free if you order it online, costs a few euro if you get it on the spot. You have to pick it up at the ski-pass office in any event, as a picture is taken on site.

DISABLED TRAVELLERS

All new public buildings are obliged to provide facilities for the disabled. Historic buildings are more difficult to convert, and access difficulties still exist. Hotels that cater for the disabled are indicated in tourist board lists. Airports and railway stations provide assistance, and certain trains are equipped to transport wheelchairs. Access to town centres is allowed for cars with disabled drivers or passengers, and special parking places are reserved for them. For further information, contact the tourist board in the city of interest.

OPENING TIMES

The opening times of museums and monuments are given in the text, though they often change without warning. National museums and monuments are usually closed on Mondays. Archaeological sites generally open at 9 and close at dusk.

Some museums are closed on the main public holidays: 1 Jan, Easter, 1 May, 15 Aug and 25 Dec. Smaller museums have have suspended regular hours altogether and are now open by appointment only. Their telephone numbers are included in the text. Entrance fees vary. EU citizens under 18 and over 65 are entitled to free admission to national museums and monuments but you need to provide ID.

Churches open early in the morning (often for 6 o'clock Mass), and most are closed during the middle of the day (12–3, 4 or 5), although cathedrals and larger churches may be open throughout daylight hours. Smaller churches and oratories are often open only in the early morning, but the key can usually be found by inquiring locally. The sacristan will also show closed chapels and crypts, and a small tip should be given. Some churches now ask that sightseers do not enter during a service, but normally visitors may do so, provided they are silent and do not approach the altar in use. At all times they are expected to cover their legs and arms, and generally dress with decorum. An entrance fee is often charged for admission to treasuries, cloisters, bell-towers and so on. Lights (operated by coins) have been installed in many churches to illuminate frescoes and altarpieces. In Holy Week most of the images are covered and are on no account shown.

Shops generally open Mon–Sat 8.30/9–1 and 3.30/4–7.30/8, although larger stores and shops is bigger towns do not close for lunch.

ADDITIONAL INFORMATION

CRIME AND PERSONAL SECURITY
Pickpocketing is a widespread problem in towns all over Italy: it is always advisable not to carry valuables, and be particularly careful on public transport. Crime should be reported at once to the police or the local *carabinieri* office (found in every town and small village). A statement has to be given in order to get a document confirming loss or damage (essential for insurance claims). Interpreters are provided. For all emergencies, T: 113. The switchboard will co-ordinate the help you need. For medical assistance: T: 118.

PHARMACIES
Pharmacies (*farmacie*) are usually open Mon–Fri 9–1 & 4–7.30 or 8. A few are open also on Saturdays, Sundays and holidays (listed on the door of every pharmacy). In all towns there is also at least one pharmacy open at night (also shown on the door of every pharmacy).

PUBLIC HOLIDAYS
Italian national holidays are as follows:
1 January
Easter Sunday and Easter Monday
25 April (Liberation Day)
1 May (Labour Day)
2 June (Festa della Repubblica)
15 August (Assumption)
1 November (All Saints' Day)
8 December (Immaculate Conception)
25 December (Christmas Day)
26 December (St Stephen)
Each town keeps its patron saint's day as a holiday.

TELEPHONE AND POSTAL SERVICES
Stamps are sold at tobacconists (*tabacchi*, marked with a large white 'T') and post offices. For all calls in Italy, dial the city code (for instance, 0461 for Trento), then the telephone number. For international and intercontinental calls, dial 00 before the telephone number. The country code for Italy is +39.

TIPPING
Service charges are normally included and tipping in Italy is not routinely expected. It is normal to round up the bill and leave a few coins in appreciation.

ACCOMMODATION
A selection of hotels, chosen on the basis of character or location, is given at the end of each section of the guide. They are classified as follows: €€€€ (€900 or over),

€€€ (€350–900), €€ (€150–300) or € (€150 or under). It is advisable to book well in advance, especially between May and October; if you cancel the booking with at least 72 hours' notice you can claim back part or all of your deposit. Service charges are included in the rates. By law breakfast is an optional extra, although a lot of hotels will include it in the room price. When booking, always specify if you want breakfast or not. If you are staying in a hotel in a town, it is often more fun to go round the corner to the nearest café for breakfast.

FOOD & DRINK

RESTAURANTS

Italian food is usually good and inexpensive. Generally speaking, the least pretentious *ristorante* (restaurant), *trattoria* (small restaurant) or *osteria* (inn or tavern) provides the best value. A selection of restaurants is given at the end of each section of the guide. Prices are categorised as follows: €€€€ (€80 or more per head), €€€ (€60–80), €€ (€40–50) and € (€30 or under). Many places are considerably cheaper at midday. It is always a good idea to reserve.

Prices on the menu do not include a cover charge (shown separately, usually at the bottom of the page), which is added to the bill. The service charge (*servizio*) is now almost always automatically added at the end of the bill; tipping is therefore not strictly necessary, but a few euro are appreciated. Note that many simpler establishments do not offer a written menu.

BARS AND CAFÉS

Bars and cafés are open from early morning to late at night and serve numerous varieties of excellent refreshments that are usually taken standing up. As a rule, you must pay the cashier first, then present your receipt to the barman in order to get served. It is customary to leave a small tip for the barman. If you sit at a table the charge is usually higher, and you will be given waiter service (so don't pay first). However, some simple bars have a few tables that can be used with no extra charge, and it is always best to ask, before ordering, whether there is waiter service or not.

COFFEE

Italy is considered to have the best coffee in Europe. *Caffè* or *espresso* (black coffee) can be ordered *alto* or *lungo* (diluted), *corretto* (with a liquor), or *macchiato* (with a dash of hot milk). A *cappuccino* is an *espresso* with more hot milk than a *caffè macchiato* and is generally considered a breakfast drink. A glass of hot milk with a dash of coffee in it, called *latte macchiato* is another early-morning favourite. In summer, many drink *caffè freddo* (iced coffee).

REGIONAL CUISINE

The cuisine of the Trentino is a medley of Venetian, Lombard, and Tyrolean influences. The basic ingredients here are polenta and cheese. The most typical Trentine polenta is made from potatoes; dressed with cream, it is found in traditional dishes such as *smacafam* (baked with lard and sausage). Many dishes are hand-me-downs from the Austro-Hungarian tradition; examples include *canederli*, the Trentine version of *Knödel* (large stuffed bread dumplings), *gulasch*, smoked meat with sauerkraut, and *zelten alla trentina* (bread dough baked with eggs and dried fruit).

In Bolzano, Bressanone and the Dolomites a marked Germanic bias prevails. Distinctive dishes that can be eaten as a first or as a main course include *Gertensuppe* (barley soup with chopped speck), *Frittatensuppe* (soup with strips of omelette), *Milzschittensuppe* (served with toast with spleen spread), *Rindgulasch* (beef goulash), *Schmorbraten* (stew), *Gröstl* (boiled diced beef and boiled potatoes, sautéed), various sausages (*Würstel*) and *Speck*. The incomparable sweets of the region include strudel, *Zelten* (Christmas cake of rye bread dough with figs, dates, raisins, pine nuts and walnuts) and *Kastanientorte* (chestnut cake served with cream).

WINE

Most Italian wines take their names from the geographical area in which they are produced, the blend of grapes of which they are made, and the estate on which the grapes were grown. The best come in numbered bottles and are marked DOC (*di origine controllata*). This is Italy's *appellation controlée*, which specifies maximum yields per vine, geographical boundaries within which grapes must be grown, permitted grape varieties and production techniques. Superior even to DOC is the DOCG (*di origine controllata e garantita*), where the denomination is also guaranteed. This is not to say that DOCG wines are automatically superior to any other. The plethora of regulation inevitably runs the risk of sclerosis, and winemakers wanting to experiment with alternative grape varieties or vinification techniques found themselves barred from the DOC or DOCG classifications, and had to label their vintages IGT (*vino da tavola con indicazione geografica tipica*). IGT denotes a *vin de pays*, a wine of special regional character. This does not necessarily mean that an IGT wine is of lesser quality than a DOC. Indeed, in some cases it may be particularly interesting and many producers, frustrated by the inflexibility of the rules, have chosen to exit the DOC system. Simple *vino da tavola* is table wine. It can be excellent, but the quality is not guaranteed.

ORDERING WINES

Red wines are *vini rossi*; white wines, *vini bianchi*; rosés, *chiaretti* or *rosati*. Dry wines are *secchi*; sweet wines, *amabili* or *dolci*. *Vino novello* is new wine. Moscato and passito is wine made from grapes that have been left on the vine or dried before pressing. When ordering, remember also that many DOC wines come in versions labelled *spumante, liquoroso, recioto* and *amarone*. Spumante is the Italian equivalent of champagne and uses some of the same methods to obtain its foamy effervescence. It is much bubblier than sparkling whites such as Prosecco, which is popular both before meals and as a light dinner wine. Liquoroso means 'liqueur-like' and usually refers to dessert wines. The term *recioto* is applied to wines made from grapes that have been dried like raisins; *amarone* is the dry, mellow version of *recioto*.

The indication Trentino precedes the name in almost all the DOC wines from the vineyards in this province; in addition to Trentino Bianco and Trentino Rosso there are single-variety red, whites, and three desert wines, Moscato Giallo (also *liquoroso*), Moscato Rosa (also *liquoroso*) and Vin Santo. The denomination Valdadige (white, red, rosé, Pinot Grigio and Schiava) refers to a territory that also includes parts of the provinces of Bolzano and Verona.

Because the South Tyrol is bilingual, its wine labels are in Italian and German. The DOC wines, whose area of production embraces the entire province of Bolzano-Alto Adige, carry the designation Alto Adige after the name (in German, the term Südtiroler precedes the name). The whites produced in the Valle dell'Isarco bear the denomination Valle Isarco (or Bressanone, in German Eisacktaler).

From hills around Bolzano come the two reds Colli di Bolzano (Bozner Leiten) and Santa Maddalena. The light red Lago di Caldaro (Kalterersee) comes from the vineyards on the lake of the same name. Terlano (Terlaner) is a white wine produced east of Bolzano. The denomination Valdadige or Etschtaler covers territory which extends into the provinces of Trento and Verona.

Acquiring good wines is easier thanks to the Strada del Vino. The South Tyrolean Wine Road begins in Nalles/Nals and meanders through Überetsch (Upper-Adige) and Unterland (Lower-Adige) until it reaches Salorno/Salurn (*see www.suedtiroler-weinstrasse.it/english/towns*). Here you can taste and buy renowned wines like the spicy white Gewürtztraminer (from Termeno/Tramin), the light red Lago di Caldaro (from the shores of the beautiful lake between Trento and Bolzano), or the full bodied Blauburgunder (Pinot Noir) and Lagrein Dunkel (an exquisite native variety that descends from Teroldego and is related to Syrah, Pinot Noir and Dureza). In the Trentino the finest wines, made from the autochthonous grapes Teroldego and Marzemino, come from the alluvial plain of the River Adige, respectively north and south of Trento. Both are full-bodied reds: Teroldego tends to be spicy and Marzemino, fruity. Other wines commonly produced in this area are Cabernet, Chardonnay, Edelvernatsch, Grauvernatsch, Lagrein Rosé, Merlot, Moscato Giallo, Müller Thurgau, Pino Bianco, Pinot Grigio, Riesling, St Magdalener and Sauvignon.

Here as elsewhere in the world vintners have embraced the fashion of creating beautiful new cellars and retail facilities. The very short list that follows represents a few of those who have given a firm philosophical basis to their endeavours.

CALDARO/KALTERN (*map B, B3*)

Manincor Winery. On a certified biodynamic estate where sustainability is paramount, Count Michael Goëss-Enzenberg asked architects Walter Angonese (Caldaro) and Rainer Köberl (Innsbruck) to design a winery entirely hidden under the vines. The architecture, with its skewed walls, echoes the topography of the vineyards. The three underground floors house large wooden casks, barrels, fermentation tanks, special presses, a bottling plant and an area for storing the bottled wine. The cellar, barely visible beneath the vineyard, is made of cast concrete mixed with organic substances that change the colour and the physical properties of the surface to match the weathered walls of the vineyard. A smart ventilation system produces just the right amount of moisture (more for the barrels, less for the bottle storage), and the temperature is regulated by a heat exchange system that reaches down 80m below the surface to maintain an ideal climate in each sector of the cellar. The estate produces fifteen different wines, all marked by character and individuality. *San Giuseppe al Lago 4, T: 0471 960230, www.manincor.com.*

Winecenter. The striking new Wine Centre, a retail outlet for the Caldaro Winegrowers' Cooperative, is actually a renovation encompassing several earlier buildings. The ingenious structure you see today was obtained by the Viennese architecture firm feld72 (2006) by enclosing the older buildings in a single envelope of coloured concrete reinforced with fibreglass. Walking around the interior is like driving down the Wine Road: you wind your way from the general sales area and wine bar, on the ground floor, to the tasting room at the building's highest level. The focus, of course, is on Lago di Caldaro/Kalterersee wines. *Via Stazione 7, T: 0471 9 6067, www.winecenter.it.*

NALLES / NALS *(map B, B2)*
Cantina Nalles Magrè/Nals Margreid. Amidst the vineyards and orchards of the Adige valley, almost half-way between Bolzano and Merano, is Markus Scherer's beautiful Nals Margreid Cellar (2011). The cooperative winery of the growers here had grown into a chaotic jumble of buildings over the years, and the desire to expand wine production demanded a more rational arrangement. The response was to build a new structure for unloading and pressing grapes, a large underground cellar that connects to the pre-existing cellar and a new barrique cellar in the courtyard, all under a large origami-like roof. The whole edifice stands on a reddish-brown coloured-concrete foundation that forms a visual and material continuum with the perimeter wall of the adjacent cemetery and with the porphyry rock of the ridge top behind it. The barrique cellar is treated as a giant wine crate made entirely made of wood. If one counts classic wines, crus and special wines, there are about two dozen Nals Margreids to taste. *Via Heiligenberg 2, T: 0471 678626, www.kellerei.it.*

MEZZOCORONA *(map A, B2)*
Cittadella del Vino. This, the largest complex dedicated to wine in Europe, has cellars for vinification and bottling, a retail space, auditorium, exhibition hall and offices. It covers over 12 acres along a front of 500m, creating a glass wall along the western edge of the valley's Rotaliana vineyards. The design, by Venetian architects Ceccheto & Associati, aspires to show that a large industrial complex can indeed be built in relative harmony with the surrounding landscape. It's easily the most interesting building in Mezzocorona, a sprawling modern town at the confluence of the Noce and the Adige. The selection of outstanding terroir wines is every bit as vast and impressive as the architecture. The Mezzacorona group includes several producers; it was formed by the 1970 merger between the Cantina Sociale (established in 1904) and the Lega fra Viticoltori (established in 1911), the first merger in Italy between two cooperatives. Here you'll find just about all the types of wine made in the Trentino-Alto Adige. A highlight is the Rotari collection of sparkling whites. *Via Tonale 110–SS 43 Val di Non, T: 0461 616300/1, www.gruppomezzacorona.it.*

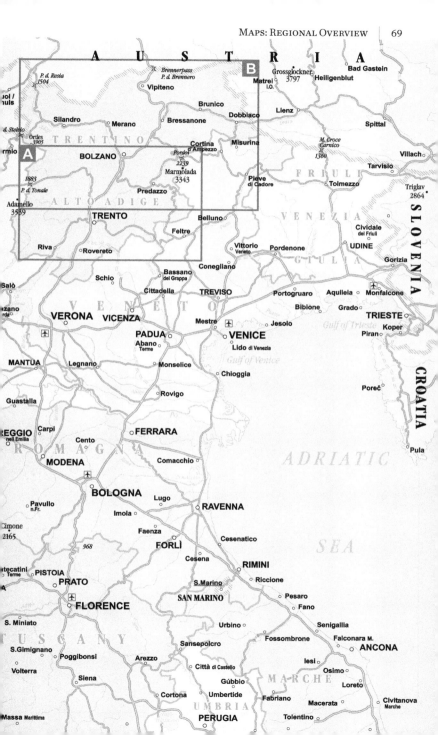

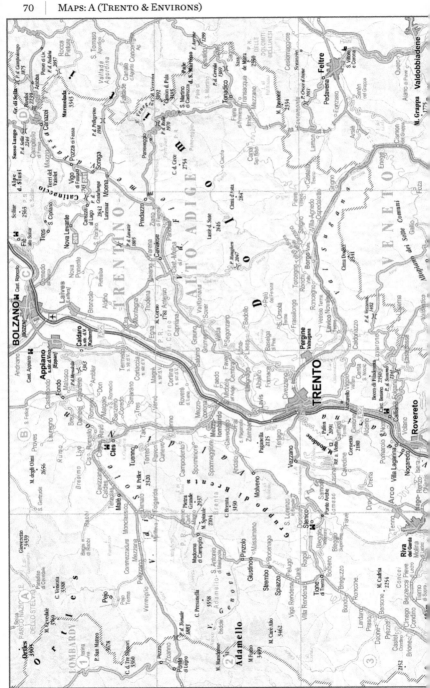

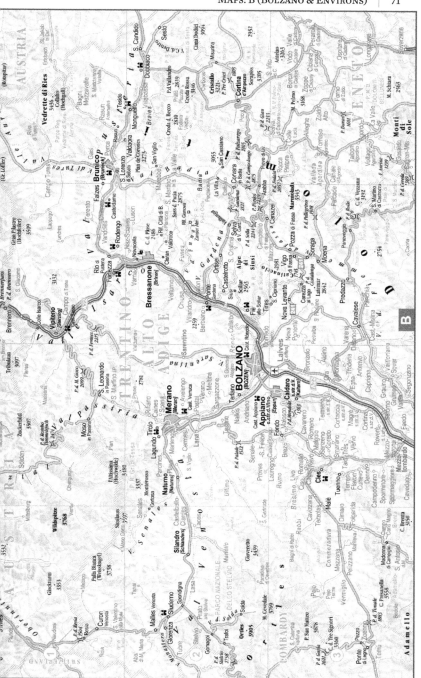

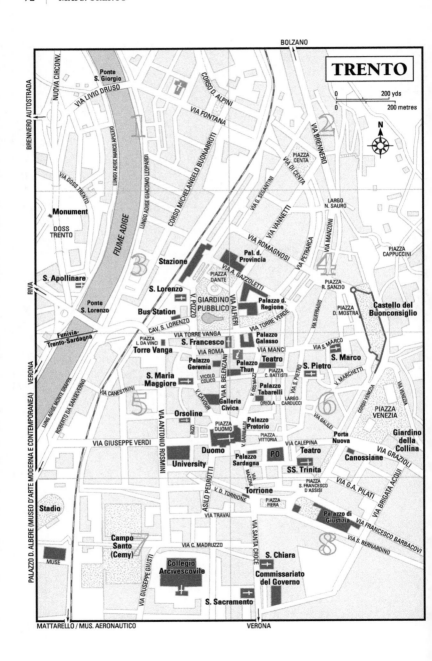

CPSIA information can be obtained
at www.ICGtesting.com
Printed in the USA
BVHW041541230222
629897BV00007B/336

9 781905 131655